Love
A Manual for Humanity

Anastacia Dadashpour

Love

A Manual for Humanity

Anastacia Dadashpour

As You Wish Publishing Phoenix, Arizona

All rights reserved. No part of this book may be reproduced or transmitted in any form or by any means, electronic or mechanical, including photo-copying, recording, or any information storage and retrieval system, without written permission from the author, exceptfor the inclusion of brief quotations in a review.

Copyright © 2021 As You Wish Publishing

ISBN 13 - 978-1-951131-33-3

Library of Congress Control Number: 2021917406

Published in the United States of America

For more information, visit the publisher's website at: www.asyouwishpublishing.com.

Cover photo credit: SV Gaia Khan

No part of this book is a substitute for mental or physical health. If you need help please seek it.

Love...

What is it? A feeling, trust, respect, longing, a partner, a playmate, a mirror, a fan, a lover, a friend.

What purpose does it serve? Do we need it? Why?

Love is the feeling of bliss, a force, a passage of trans-formation, awakening, self-awareness and content-ment. It is an invitation to live in joy and enhance the world through which we walk.

This book is about accessing Love as a tool to higher consciousness, peace, synchronicity, and manifestation. Love is something that each of us has experienced in some capacity, and in accessing the feeling of love, we can use it as a conduit of change.

If, for a moment, we can suppose that the universe is conspiring to support each of us as the blossoms of its creation, what would be standing in the way of our truest potential?

Ourselves!

Yes, each of us has constructed creative, often unconscious, ways to lure ourselves away from our greatest potential.

"Our deepest fear is not that we are inadequate. Our deepest fear is that we are powerful beyond measure. It is our Light, not our Darkness that most frightens us. Love is what we are born with. Fear is what we learned here." ~ Marianne Williamson

Gratefully, each of us is equipped with an undying umbilical cord to Divine Source, Love.

You can't argue with Love. It is a force that has no restriction beyond our personal constructs. One that is alive, a constant universal energy, something that binds all of creation together. It has no interest other than our perfect wellbeing. The force of Love is not judgmental or punitive. It is wholly, absolutely supportive. If we attune to it, it will support our drive towards our greatest potential, which ultimately leads us back to Love.

If you can access your memories of unconditional Love, such as the first time you saw your baby, the first time you made love with your dearest beloved, a sweet and simple crush that you had as a youth, immense gratitude for a special gift received, an experience with a spiritual figure or practice, a moment in nature that transported you into deep appreciation, or into experiencing something so vast or beautiful it commanded absolute awe or appreciation. If you can harness any of those feelings and focus one of them into and onto different experiences in your life, you can access a deeper command of your happiness and wellbeing.

I have intentionally used repetition in this text to provide a range of access points to the feeling of Love. It is my hope that of the array of examples, explanations and practices that I provide, at least one will offer a profound awakening and awareness of the depth and expanse of Love. Each of these lessons is a spoke of a wheel in which the center is Love. At times, I intermingle the words Love, Source and Divine. You do not need to subscribe to any specific belief or tradition to practice the exercises that I have laid out in this book. I only mention the origin of some of these practices to acknowledge and give context to where they were developed.

This book is a guide to assist all who desire to live more fully in this flow of divine universal Love. This process will not require that you change anything in your life other than how you feel. Any changes will happen naturally as your experience of Love increases. However, it will take a bit of concentration, dedication, and focus. Anyone can do this. And what a better world it would be for all of us to live in if teachers, parents, Wall Street executives and politicians walked through their lives emitting and feeling a greater depth of Love, living IN Love.

This guide is not about romantic love between two people. That is too often conditional Love. This is about tapping into the flow of infinite Love. In this book, I will illustrate 38 different lessons to access this force. Once you can identify the feeling of unconditional Love, you will be asked to concentrate on that until you can feel it long enough to superimpose that feeling onto circumstances that are present for you now. First, you will be asked to bathe in this Love, your Love, the kind that only you know how to give and receive. What does that Love feel like? Can you give and receive it without restriction, without the stories you have created for yourself, like the innocence and childlike nature of Love? A child that has no attachment to the Love it receives, he or she who just knows what Love feels like and gravitates to its warmth, safety and power? You are an inescapable part of the source of Love. Can you allow yourself to surrender to receiving Love from this eternal well? If you can bathe in that Love for a moment, what would it feel like to walk in that Love throughout your day and in all aspects of your life? What would it feel like to actively be a conduit for Love in all of the moments of your existence?

To do this does not depend on your own capacity for love, your own goodness, strength or discipline. This is an array of practices that ask you to tap into a force far greater, richer, and deeper than anything that you individually can attain or harness. You already have the innate awareness, understanding and capacity to attain complete Love. It already exists inside of all of us. Each of us already has the blueprint for accessing Love; it is your most elemental state of being.

This process of tuning into Love creates profound synchronicity and the power of manifestation by attracting the beauty and harmony that is magnetized to Love, which can show up as a person, a situation, a dynamic, or as healing the cause of discomfort or addiction.

Albert Einstein wrote in a letter to his daughter: "There is an extremely powerful force that, so far, science has not found a formal explanation to. It is a force that includes and governs all others and is even behind any phenomenon operating in the universe and has not yet been identified by us. This universal force is Love…This force explains everything and gives meaning to life. This is the variable that we have ignored for too long, maybe because we are afraid of love because it is the only energy in the universe that man has not learned to drive at will."

Love is certainly the most powerful force in an individual's subterranean universe.

This is not in any way about opening old wounds or dissecting pain. What is, IS. Love heals all and is one of the most essential, powerful, and authentic expressions that conscious human beings can experience.

This book is not about the science that will validate this process. There is a wealth of information on the topic of consciousness being influenced by Love. Please investigate it, as it is fascinating. **The objective of this book is to give you concrete examples of how to access, hold and implement Love in your life.** This is a process that you can explore to bring more light, joy, compassion, and harmony into our shared world.

The goal is to achieve the highest sustained level of bliss in your life as the key to accessing the greatest expression of your own unique potential in the world. Once we live inside of Love and can vibrate that into our personal landscapes and the world, we can collectively shift away from fear-consciousness, scarcity, jealousy and domination into love-consciousness of cooperation, abundance, support and mutual empowerment. I hope to see the expansion of Love as a tool to combat hate, hostility and intolerance globally.

About the Author

In 2008 I mourned the unnatural death of my first-born child, Azaria. The experience shattered me to the core. However, the experience of being shattered open was one that has given me the opportunity to experience Love in a deeper way than I had ever previously imagined. Marking the first anniversary of her death, I realized that I had a choice: I could continue to live as the miserable, angry and despondent person I had become, or I could choose to change my understanding of the experience. I didn't like myself, and I imagine not many people did. My heart was as cold, dark and dense as coal. I made a conscious decision to become the person that I once was: happy, curious and generous of spirit. I realized that I owed it to Azaria to be a strong, capable and caring mother to her even in her death. So, I began to direct my attention to the beauty that I saw in the world. It was slow at first, but I committed to it with my whole being. I put effort towards appreciating the goodness in my life and giving that my attention. It seemed as though the more I focused on the silver linings, the less dark life felt. Over time I started doing yoga again, repeating mantras that reminded me of the life I wanted to live into. I focused on giving Love to others and redeveloping the capacity to receive it. My husband and I had our second daughter Izabela, and I expanded my capabilities to Love even further. I was able to parent two beloved children, one seen and one unseen.

Since that time, I have continued to experience a series of ego deaths. With each new discarded and discovered layer, I was forced to merge and mingle my past perceptions with the profound new insights into divine Love. These newfound states of awareness allowed me to feel so open and vulnerable that it almost hurt. It sometimes felt edgy, alienating, and uncomfortable. Yet I was somehow blown open in a way that was undeniably true and sweet. I tapped into a force so strong that I couldn't have begun to fight it even if I had tried. I felt like a portal came out of my heart, allowing me to see with Love, feel with Love, and just simply be in the experience of Love.

My point here is that with a heart shattered open, I have learned to access and direct Love in my life to the point where synchronicity is the norm. I wake up and rest each day feeling surrounded by transformational Love. I now understand that each of us has the capacity for this kind of union in Love.

Throughout my life, I have been acutely interested in justice, poverty and the human condition. As a young woman, my curiosity led me to travel around the world, exploring its people, customs, languages, religions, landscapes, politics, economies and cultural norms. After many years of accumulating insight and life experience, I was inspired to return to school to study journalism. I believed that through a better understanding of one another's humanity, we would inevitably veer towards respect. Young and idealistic at the time, yes, but this is still my aspiration for humanity today as we move inextricably into a global society. Beyond the fact that we are all alive here on Earth together at the same time, what are our shared commonalities? Love is the overarching answer to this question; it is a universally recognized force that binds each of us to the other and to all creation.

While completing my graduate degree at the Josef Korbel School of International Studies, I dedicated the majority of my work towards investigating international human rights, conflict resolution and democratization in the

Middle East. As fascinating as all of these topics are in theory and practice, I invariably asked myself: "How is humanity able to curb suffering, alienation and violence? How can we create a new paradigm to collectively address the causes of these ailments instead of ameliorating them once they have been experienced? What connects us despite our differences? What makes us the same? What can we agree is important? What is something that we all share?" Love is the answer.

I invite you to use the experience of Love to change your life. Since allowing myself to be a conduit of Love, I have noticed 1) a powerful sense of community, both in the quality and quantity of inspiring individuals who are harnessing and radiating Love as well as making impactful choices for themselves and the whole of humanity 2) synchronicity beyond my ability to explain it and 3) the quality of my experience in life and my interactions with all that exist.

The more I stay in a state of Love, the more amazed I am by how easy life can be. It is as though Love is a conduit of synchronicity. Through its magnetism, life is seemingly conspiring to support me. All of the experiences I've had in my life have been training for the experiences I'm having now.

For instance, I ended up in Jerusalem on Orthodox Easter with countless pilgrims from around the world on May 1st, 2016. I was told via email correspondence by a woman I had not yet met to stay in the Azaria hotel. Azaria is the name of my first daughter, who was born on April 25th and passed on May 1. I was not planning to go to

Jerusalem on this trip or to be there on this date for this occasion. So, to stay at the Azaria hotel on my daughter's death day in the holiest of cities, with pilgrims from around the world who had come to commemorate the resurrection of Jesus, felt like a series of miraculous events.

Another example of inexplicable alignment was when one New Year's morning, I woke up to a compelling desire to send an unsolicited, detailed letter to an organization I admired with ideas about how they could improve their outreach to include more members. This email led to my being invited by my favorite Graduate School professor to sit on the organization's board. I was welcomed and supported in creating a committee to do what I had proposed, which has opened up a world of possibilities in my life.

You are a change agent for humanity!

In conjunction with education, communication, economic equality and enlightened politics, my deepest hope is that all of these actions are conducted with a far more profound element of Love in their delivery. Each of us is both an actor and a director in this experiment that we call life. If we can redirect and experience our lives to contain more Love, we can collectively shift the paradigm into a global society where Love is both the cause and the effect.

We are born of universal Love. Our deepest longing is to be reunited with it by sharing our unique gifts, talents and assets.

This is a very dynamic time for our planet and its populations. This is a time that could be experienced in anxious anticipation or in focused, intentional, devotional Love of ourselves, each other, humanity and our life-giving planet. This is the time that we must consciously and deliberately actualize Love as a tool and solution in the quest for a new paradigm.

As the author Arthur Ward once said, "If you can imagine it, you can achieve it; if you can dream it, you can become it." Is it possible for each of us to combat treachery and its causes while uplifting its victims through the way we direct our consciousness, handle our jobs and treat each other on a daily basis? It is a question that may be difficult to answer, but there is no failure in trying.

Each of the lessons is a different invitation to connect to Love. Although the lessons do build on each other, they are not in any particular order. The primary goal is to meet this book with an open mind and a willingness to open your heart. Please be prepared to surrender to your highest knowing. This awareness can brilliantly serve you, your relations, and society.

The Devotion is meant to set the tone and intention for the Concept. I suggest that you read out loud to yourself (or to your partner, if you have one for the exercise), making clear in your mind your intention for the exercise. The Concept is to provide you with an explanation of what will be explored in the Practice. Read the Concept to yourself slowly and carefully, focusing on how the words resonate within you, especially in your body. The Practice is the action you will take to train your awareness to tune into

Love. You can do this exercise as many times as you want. Try staying in contemplation of each of these practices for a week. Consider setting aside an hour once a week to do the initial practice and carry it with you throughout the week.

This work was primarily inspired by insights that came through my dreamtime and the liminal space between sleep and wakefulness.

Lessons

Lesson 1 I See You 1

Lesson 2 Melt... 5

Lesson 3 Love is Yours... 9

Lesson 4 Ego the Trickster, What is it Keeping
from You? 13

Lesson 5 Unconditional Love 15

Lesson 6 Perceiving Through Your Chakras 23

Lesson 7 Introspection, Truth and Self-Awareness 29

Lesson 8 Healing Yourself.. 33

Lesson 9 You are a Love-Powered Super(s)hero 37

Lesson 10 Conscious Communication.............................. 39

Lesson 11 Love as a Meditation 43

Lesson 12 Unify in Love... 47

Lesson 13 How We Live in This Moment is
How We Set the Course for the Future 51

Lesson 14 Intuition and Magnetism Follow Your Flow ... 55

Lesson 15 Love Is So Much More Than Attraction 59

Lesson 16 Letting Go... 63

Lesson 17 Forgiveness... 67

Lesson 18 Non-Judgement... 71

Lesson 19 Beauty... 77

Lesson 20 Looking into the Shadows 79

Lesson 21 Love is Universal Consciousness 83

Lesson 22 100 Monkeys 87

Lesson 23 Gratitude 91

Lesson 24 Active Love Affects Our Consciousness, Communities and Planet 95

Lesson 25 Love, Joy and Prayer 99

Lesson 26 Falling in Love with Your Beloved Even if You Haven't Yet Met 103

Lesson 27 Devotion 105

Lesson 28 Lineage, Evolution & Love 109

Lesson 29 Tolerance & Justice 113

Lesson 30 Shedding Layers 119

Lesson 31 Spirals of Refinement and Release 121

Lesson 32 Fear as a Guide 125

Lesson 33 Love Does Not Need to be Passive Love Can Be Fierce 129

Lesson 34 Community 135

Lesson 35 Balance of Tension 139

Lesson 36 I Am Enough 143

Lesson 37 Overcoming the Separation of the Masculine and Feminine 147

Lesson 38 Heartbreak 151

Epilogue 155

Additional Resources 159

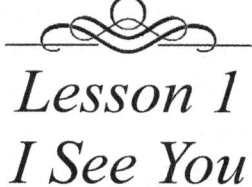

Lesson 1
I See You

Inspiration

I see the Infinite in you. Your eyes are a portal into universal Love. As I lean into the nourishment of your essence, I allow myself to feel safe here. I am Love in your presence. In my abandonment of identification with you as an individual, I see you in your true nature, as a vessel of Love.

Concept

What does it feel like to be seen? To really be seen. If you look in the mirror and meet your own gaze, whom do you see? If someone else were to sincerely try to see you, would you let yourself show up in all of your magnificence and insecurity? Could you allow yourself to be vulnerable enough to let someone else see all of who you are? The truth is it doesn't matter what anyone else sees or experiences when they look at you. This practice is to allow yourself to be exactly who you are in your unique perfection. This is not about asking anyone else to accept you, but for allowing yourself to accept all of who you are, as only you know who that is. Only you know the depth and gravity of your inner landscapes. No one else can, should, or will validate that for you. You must see yourself, with the lens of the Love of your own unconditional heart. You can hide from others, but it only creates personal suffering to hide from yourself. Allowing others to see you is a reflection of how much you are willing to be seen. The depth of your vulnerability equates to the full extent of courage.

What does it feel like to let yourself be seen? This was very difficult for me. When I really confronted the question, it felt uncomfortably vulnerable, and I wasn't sure how to cope with its uneasiness. Just keep opening your mind and heart and asking the question—what does it feel like to let yourself be seen?

Remember, you are not asking for validation from another person. You are asking that another act as a reflection for you to see yourself.

This experiment is for you to know that through your vulnerability, you are safe enough to be held in Love. During the process, you will realize that you are a vastly more profound person than you have ever previously acknowledged. We all are. By recognizing that you have been living in the shadow of yourself, you will gain the capacity to see yourself in an entirely new light. You will be able to see yourself more fully. Perhaps you have been hiding behind past beliefs and experiences of the person you imagine others perceive you to be. Perhaps you find these frameworks merely create the shell of who you are. Your deeper self is a source of untapped potential. This understanding is not to serve your ego. Stepping into and owning the brilliance of who you truly are amplifies the collective. This is not a solitary or isolated story. We all have the key to unlock that door if we allow our ego to step aside and receive the profound awareness that we are all born of exquisitely unique potential. It is up to each of us to allow this great potential to be seen and recognized in order to be actualized and utilized. You may just find that once you are able to tap this potential and live in it, the world around you will begin to reflect your radiance right back to you.

When you look at someone, with or without them knowing, acknowledge to yourself, "I see you." Give yourself the opportunity to see them beyond the judgement of your perception. Ultimately, you will recognize how similar we all are.

How has it served you not to have been seen? Does that story still have a place in your life? Can you transform that story?

Practice

There is value in practicing vulnerability by asking someone to do this exercise with you. This does not need to be done with a romantic partner but can be anyone you trust to take the practice seriously. If there is someone with whom you can share this, it is helpful to get some external reflection.

Even if you do not have a partner to do this with, it can be equally powerful to do this practice by yourself. To see yourself in the mirror in this way is quite revealing. The exchange of words is not necessary or suggested during eye gazing.

Give yourself at least one minute the first time. Ten minutes is ideal.

Look into the eyes of the person across from you and see them without their story. Look at them without judgement. Just gently notice who they are. If you have judgement, notice what that is and what space it is holding between you. Imagine that you are two portals of light, that's all. Gaze at each other with no expectation. Just acknowledge that you are each a portal of light, illuminating and reflecting radiance upon one another. See beyond their shell, into the infinite that exists within them. See them without their story, just as two portals looking deeply into each other, without any preconceived expectation.

What do you see? Allow yourself to see them for who they truly are.

This practice can change the vibration of Love that currently exists in a relationship.

By seeing beyond the illusion of one's shell, you can practice this in your daily life by looking at each person you encounter as a vastly more complex, innocent and divine being.

Lesson 2
Melt

Inspiration

Imagine a waterfall. Now picture that waterfall as an infinite flow of pure Love. Let your attachment to fear and worry wash away as though this never-ending waterfall of Love is pouring over you. The waterfall will continue to cleanse you of that which no longer serves you, as long as you choose to stay in its flow. Let yourself bathe in this flow and imagine it seeping into and clearing every pore of your being. It is your choice to be in this cleansing, to part with old, outdated, unwanted patterning.

Unnecessary thoughts are a hindrance, which the emergent you no longer has time or space for. That which you let go of can be as specific or broad as you choose. That which you no longer need to hold onto will be washed away downstream and dissipate. If it no longer serves you, let it go.

Visualize making more room to receive Love by flushing out outdated, unneeded patterns that no longer serve you, then filling that space with divine Love. You can now show up in relationship to the divine with greater capacity for the infinite possibilities that reside in the universal flow of Love.

Concept

This can be done with a partner, a family member, a friend, or an imaginary partner. This has nothing to do with any shared past experiences, although it requires someone you can let yourself be vulnerable to, someone you feel safe with. Each partner will hold space for the other for as long as the person being held requires. Don't put a time limit on the process so that each person can fully allow themselves to unwind into this experience and garner all its benefits. The person holding space needs to be as calm and present as possible, remembering that for these moments, he or she is in service of the receiver.

I once had an experience in which the person holding space for me had a breakthrough and spontaneously overcame his fear of not being enough for someone else. As soon as he acknowledged this and realized he was enough for me in the moment, he was able to be even more present with me, which allowed me to surrender even more deeply. He said that when he shifted how much he was able to be present, that is when my tears began to flow. He held me in a way that I was able to completely allow myself to receive. The embrace was so potent that I broke like a dam. My body convulsed with all of the pent-up emotion that was ready to be released. It flooded out, without shame or hesitation. I felt held and to surrender into that knowing was powerful. Our relationship wasn't in any way romantic, but we both stayed committed to the practice and totally engaged in the present moment.

You might experience some sort of heartfelt release, perhaps one that is neither painful nor joyous. It may arrive as a feeling of being held without the expectation of needing to do anything other than receive the gift of being held.

Practice

What does it feel like to melt into someone else's arms? Allow yourself to be held without feeling obligated to do, say, or be anything other than what you are in that moment. See how far into surrender you can go. See what it feels like to let yourself be held without any attachment to what was in the past or what lies in the future. In this moment, you are safe and can let yourself surrender to the Love and support of someone else.

Why might letting go of someone else's physical presence be scary? The voluntary release of control is often a new and difficult territory to explore. Vulnerability is challenging. What are we giving up by being vulnerable? Are we actually giving anything up, or are we gaining a greater sense of awareness and capacity to feel? As we allow our awareness to shift away from control and containment, we allow space for the possibility of Love, peace, presence and fulfillment.

What does it take for you to melt, to fully let go? What do you think it would take for you to trust that someone else will catch you?

Scan your body to see where you are holding tension. Feel that tension you are holding. Now give yourself permission to let that tension go. Relax. Allow your mind to relax. Feel the tension in your body give way to someone else's embrace.

Try it, see how far you can go. Then try it again. The good news is that this practice takes nothing but time and willingness. Practice… That's why yogis and meditators call their efforts a "Practice." Results and rewards come with practice.

How does someone else know that you have melted? Notice if the energy has shifted for either one of you or both. You can ask if anything in your partner's awareness has changed.

How does it feel to have surrendered into someone else's present and supportive embrace? Once you have found a satisfying level of release, try to deeply recognize what that feels like. Once you can recognize this feeling, you can access it again and again. That vulnerability is not dependent on anyone else. Now that you have recognized that feeling, it is yours to revisit whenever you are called to do so. That softening is a doorway to access greater depths of Love on many levels.

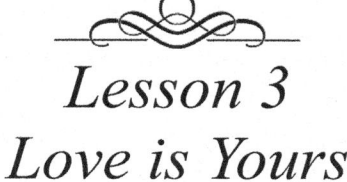

Lesson 3
Love is Yours

Inspiration

Repeat the mantra Love and Joy with the full force of your intention as many times as you can per day until these energies permeate every aspect of your being. Become a walking manifestation of Peace and Love, radiating the truest meaning of these words out into the world beyond your physical being.

Concept

I began saying the mantra of Love and Joy during a period of deep turbulence in my life with my husband. I began repeating it probably hundreds of times a day, when I was driving, brushing my teeth, in line at the grocery store, in bed before sleep, etc. It became almost a default thought for me. My partner and I did eventually separate and divorce, but we have done it with such deep Love, grace and mutual respect that we have even amazed ourselves and each other with the ease in which we have transitioned into a new relationship as co-parents. I believe this mantra has also set the stage for at least some of the profound Love and Joy I have experienced in the years since. The mantra Love and Joy is a reminder that we have the capacity to reshape how we experience the world that we live in.

The possibility of this new paradigm can replace transactional Love with unconditional Love. We all must be able to experience Love. I can't think of a situation in our complex world of human existence where Love, acceptance and appreciation are not fundamentally part of the remedy.

Practice

What does it feel like to fall in Love, to be giddy and bursting with joy? That experience is as unique as each pair of individuals who fashion it. In this practice, you get to direct the scene, paint the picture, sculpt the form. This is your creation. Your imagination can make it as serious or as silly as you desire it to be, as long as you are able to access the feeling of being fully met in Love.

Let your heart blossom in the paradise of Love. There is no one in your imagination to judge you or make you into anything other than the perfect reflection of Love that you are in this instant. You are invited into a space beyond being, where Love is all that exists. Here you will find the essence of what you wish to bring back into your ordinary reality. Smell it, feel it, breathe it in, feel it inside of every pore of your being. Soak it up as though there are no limits. You have just created a portal where Love exists. If this Love is real in your heart, can you imagine sharing this magnificent sensation with another? You may know who this individual is, or you may hold this yet unknown being in your heart's imagination. This person need not have a face or a body. You are simply tapping into the essence of where you choose to be met. By holding the feeling of Love without conditions, you are inviting your vibrational match to find you here.

I invite you to delve into this blissful feeling of unfathomable Love and linger here for as long as you can. Don't attach a story or an outcome to the feeling. Just stay with it and notice the sensations that it musters. Immerse yourself fully in the feeling of being with a person who adores you and whom you adore. Luxuriate in the feeling of giving, receiving and being inside of unconditional Love. Love is the container that holds you. You are developing a muscle, and, as with any muscle, it must be trained to be strengthened.

Lesson 4
Ego the Trickster, What is it Keeping from You?

Inspiration

"Love is a process in which ego is lost, and infinity is experienced." ~ Yogi Bhajan

Concept

I think of the ego as the proverbial mischievous angel on one shoulder trying to distract me, while my higher self is the angel on the opposing shoulder directing me to who I really am. Neither is wrong, and both play important roles. However, the ego is like a prankster and relies on your cooperation to keep it in business. It does not want you to know your true nature because the more you do, the less power it has over you. The more it is fed, the larger it gets, and the more control it has in directing matters. The more you let it distract you, the more power it has over you, like a positive feedback loop. The more attention you pay to your higher self, the less attention you give the ego, allowing your higher self to influence and guide you with increasing precision. Your higher self is the part of you that wants you to clearly see the authentic nature of reality.

Even the horrors of war, the loss of beloveds, belongings, and time cannot take away our choice to be in alignment with the connective power of Love.

Practice

Imagine who you are when you are stripped of your title, your attachments, your ethnicity, language, society, familial ties and imprints. These are the things that the ego finds important. And as all of these things hold some measure of importance in our everyday life, they are not as important to us as we break the bonds of attachment and suffering. Words and complexities dissolve, and life boils down to its simplest, most basic form. Ask yourself the following questions, keeping in mind that while your ego dissolves, your higher self allows Love to seep increasingly deeper into your consciousness. If the purest, clearest essence of yourself were to answer these questions, what would it say? Give yourself pause after each question to breathe into it, open your mind and your heart to the question and the answer, as though opening a vault of cherished secrets. This is your investigation. Only you have the answers. If the answers don't come to you, ask again. Hold the question inside of you. Explore it. Don't allow judgment to creep in. Notice what comes up. The answer may be a riddle.

What is your ego keeping hidden from you?

What does it not want you to find?

If you let go of your ego, by no longer letting it direct your life, what would happen?

If you let your higher-self guide your actions, what would happen?

Lesson 5
Unconditional Love

Inspiration

The following Meta meditation is offered by WiseMindBody. You can find the 13-minute Loving Kindness Meditation by following this link:

https://youtu.be/-d_AA9H4z9U

"Allow yourself to get comfortable, relax your shoulders, relax your eyes, relax your jaw. You can be seated or lying down for this meditation. Today we will be exploring Meta or Loving Kindness.

Through this meta meditation, we will be exploring the cultivation of feelings of compassion. Feelings of Loving Kindness for yourself and for others. So, allow yourself to relax and notice how your breath feels right now. Simply watch your breath. Notice the texture of your breathing. Notice the rate of your breathing. Notice the depth of your breathing. There's no need to change it. Just observe.

Bring awareness to your chest, to your heart. Place your awareness there as you continue to watch your breath. Notice what it feels like to breathe into your chest, to breathe into your heart. Simply place all of your awareness right there in the center of your chest.

Now slowly and silently repeat this phrase in your mind: may I be happy, may I be well, may I be comfortable and at peace. May I be happy, may I be well, may I be comfortable and at peace. Continue to repeat these words in your mind and heart. Notice any subtle changes that occur and how you feel. May I be happy, may I be well, may I be comfortable and at peace. Continue to breathe into your heart. Continue to repeat those words. May I be happy, may I be well, may I be comfortable and at peace.

Now bring into your awareness someone who you Love dearly. Notice who comes to mind. And keeping an image of this person in your mind's eye, silently repeat these words: may you be happy, may you be well, may you be comfortable and at peace. May you be happy, may you be well, may you be comfortable and at peace. May you be happy, may you be well, may you be comfortable and at peace. Notice how you feel in your chest as you continue repeating those words. May you be happy, may you be well, may you be comfortable and at peace.

Now bring into your mind more of your loved ones. Offer them that same message. That same prayer. May you be happy, may you be well, may you be comfortable and at peace. Notice how you feel right now.

Bring into your awareness people who you would consider acquaintances. Bring them into your mind's eye. And again, repeat these words: may you be happy, may you be well, may you be comfortable and at peace. May you be happy, may you be well, may you be comfortable and at peace. Notice how you feel as you extend Loving Kindness to acquaintances.

Think of someone you have a conflict with. Picture this person in your mind's eye. See if you can offer this person the same Loving Kindness that you have offered to others. May you be happy, may you be well, may you be comfortable and at peace. May you be happy, may you be well, may you be comfortable and at peace. Notice how this feels, to offer feelings of Loving Kindness to someone with whom you have conflict.

Let's expand this feeling another step further. Picture the entire human race, male and female, all nations, all cultures, all races, all colors of skin, all sexual orientations, all ages, all heights and weights, all people, all human beings. May we be happy, may we be well, may we be comfortable and at peace. May we be happy, may we be well, may we be comfortable and at peace. Notice how you feel in your heart right now. Notice what is present for you. Spend the next few moments feeling this, noticing this. Simply experiencing this feeling right here. Continue to breathe into your heart. Continue to focus your awareness right there in the center of your chest.

I invite you to open your eyes, carrying this feeling of Loving Kindness within you. Begin to wiggle your fingers and your toes. Notice how you feel in your body right now. Notice what's present. Carry this feeling of Loving Kindness with you. Carry this feeling of Loving Kindness as you interreact with others today. May you be happy, may you be well, may you be comfortable and at peace. Blessings."

Concept

Unconditional Love is unconcerned with the outcome. Think about how expansive it is to give Love, not only to the people who you perceive as deserving but to those who are in a state of dis-ease as well.

Meta meditation is devoted to Loving unconditionally, without the attachment of it being reciprocated in any way. To relinquish attachment to the results and the effects of Love is profound. This is a path to understanding the practice of unconditional Love. To know and thoroughly feel unconditional Love allows one to expand their capacity for it exponentially. If you hold onto the belief that you need to receive as much Love as you give, that places your dependence and capacity for Love on others. You could hinder your ability to give Love based on how much you perceive you are receiving, limiting you from feeling Love based on the condition of your desires being met. Why would we choose to limit the capacity of our Love, knowing that it is limitless once we disentangle it from our attachments to its outcome? Love then comes from the giving and not from the conditions surrounding it.

Why would we choose to contain boundless Love by placing narrow and defining conditions upon it? When we are non-attached, which is different from being unattached, we do not affix our feelings to the result of other people's actions. This choice of free will leads to a decrease in our own suffering and promotes unconditional Love for self and others.

Some may say that love can be a deep source of pain. Is it love, or is it the story around love that is the source of pain?

I've always loved the saying, "kill 'em with kindness." It is so simple and serves multiple purposes. First, it is intended to be a deflection of someone's anger, frustration, or hostility. Second, and perhaps most importantly, kindness is an expression of Love, and it covertly pierces the agitated person with the complete opposite energy when they are most heated, least expecting, and in a moment when most needing to be an unsuspecting recipient of Love. Kindness is disarming. Third, this simple yet effective tactic diverts attention from the underlying cause of the conflict and presents the antagonist(s) with two options: anger or kindness. Regardless of what the struggle is about, the spirit of generosity expressed in the gesture of kindness will always be the more righteous and victorious approach. Fourth, it provides a means to dissolve hostility and provide a replacement in the form of something that can repair communication. We've probably all heard the saying, "Love heals all." Finally, by not taking on someone else's frustration and simply offering kindness, you haven't succumbed to the agitation. You are able to stay above it, free from the barbs of someone else's projection. And while doing so, you are lifting up another at a time when he or she may need it.

Practice

What would it feel like to walk through your day, holding Love as your primary state of consciousness? How would it affect all those around you? Your relationships? How would this affect your ego? (Hint, your ego feeds off of conflict to define itself and strives to be right!) What if Love was more essential than being right, being powerful or being important? What if you were free of any preconceptions regarding your Love and the outcomes that giving your Love may produce? What would it feel like to give up the idea of what Love should look like?

I once had a beautiful and instantaneous connection to a woman sitting next to me on a plane. She shared many things about her life, one of which was that she was unable to let go of her last relationship. By the end of the flight, I suggested, "Why don't you bless him in the new Love that he has found and Love him from a place of non-attachment?" Somehow it struck a chord, and she began writing down ideas. She told me that in shifting her ability to Love her past partner as he was versus how she continued to desire him to be, it freed her from the longing of wanting to be in the relationship with him. It was her attachment that needed to dissolve, which was entirely up to her to enact. She believed this awareness would give her the freedom to let him go in Love and move on in her life. I shared in the joy of her revelation, and I believe that we were serendipitously placed next to each other in the sky in order to find that truth.

A foundational principle of Buddhist teachings is that non-attachment leads to a decrease in suffering. What would it feel like to establish a practice of giving Love without the attachment of receiving it back, meeting each moment in the flow of Love and emotional insight?

Many of the great spiritual leaders have suggested that mastery over oneself is not letting others' life experiences disrupt our personal equanimity.

Lesson 6
Perceiving Through Your Chakras

Inspiration

Take big, deep breaths into your belly. Feel it rising and expanding. Know that it is full and open. Now imagine that breath going into your heart and up into the sky above you and down through your legs into the earth below you. Acknowledge that you are in the center of the earth and sky. Both are available to support you now and at all times. Imagine this flow of deep breaths moving energy through your body for a few minutes. You can start with a dedication of one minute. See how this feels and each time you practice, increase your awareness for an additional minute. The most important thing to remember is to be present inside in the breath. The quality of your presence is paramount. The more that you can be totally inside of the present moment, the better. Make the present moment your principal focus. With every inhalation, feel your heart opening, and with every exhalation, feel your heart softening. See how malleable and receptive you can make it.

Concept

What would it feel like to be a portal of divine flow, Love and inspiration? What if these qualities flowed through you like a trickle at first, and as your capacity progressively increased, grew to a torrent? What if your understanding of the world was filtered through your heart? What does the heart chakra tell us? How are we informed by the other chakras?

According to ancient Hindu belief systems, each of us has an internal system comprised of seven energy centers throughout the body called chakras. These centers of energy can be interpreted as portals of power and receptivity, each having the capability of assessing certain energies through specific points in the body.

The first or root chakra grounds you to the abundance and fertility of the earth. Muladhara, as it is called, is related to instinct, security, survival and basic human potentiality. Physically it governs sexuality, mentally it directs stability, emotionally it governs sensuality, and spiritually it guides a sense of security. It is associated with the color red.

The second or sacral chakra, Svadhishthana, is related to reproduction; mentally, it guides creativity, emotionally it governs joy, and spiritually it governs enthusiasm. It is associated with the color orange.

The third chakra or solar plexus is called Manipura. Physically it is related to digestion, mentally it guides personal power, emotionally it governs expansiveness. Spiritually, it is the center of all matters of growth. It is associated with the color yellow.

The fourth or heart chakra, Anahata, is physically related to circulation, emotionally it guides unconditional Love for the self and others, mentally it directs passion, and spiritually it governs devotion. The fourth chakra is associated with the color green.

The fifth or throat chakra, Vishuddha, physically relates to communication. Emotionally it guides independence, mentally it governs fluent thought, and spiritually, it holds one's sense of security. The fifth chakra is associated with the color blue.

The sixth or third-eye chakra, Ajna, involves balancing the higher and lower selves and trusting inner guidance. Its inner aspects relate to access to intuition. Mentally it supports visual consciousness, and emotionally it deals with clarity on an intuitive level. The sixth chakra is associated with the color indigo.

The seventh or crown chakra, Sahasrara, is considered to be the access point of pure consciousness, within which there is no separation between object and subject. Physically it fuses action with meditation, mentally it unites action with universal consciousness and unity, and emotionally it integrates action with beingness. The seventh chakra is associated with the color violet.

Each of these points in the body can offer a lens or a brain through which information is filtered. Imagine what daily life could look like for each of us if we gathered, interpreted and disseminated information through the perception of the heart. What emotional insight might we garner? Would life have greater clarity? Could we perceive more deeply what is real for us?

Practice

Give yourself some quiet time to relax. Imagine each of these seven chakra energy centers as a portal for both the inflow and outflow of information. Each of these centers has an intelligence of its own. Start with the first chakra and visualize this center blossoming open.

Ask each chakra what information it has to share with you?

What is its unique message to you?

What does it need?

Ask it to open to its highest and truest potential.

Repeat, "I open to the lessons and wisdom that reside here and ask for the capacity to hold these lessons as they become clear to me."

"I ask for the strength to incorporate these lessons into my being for the good of all."

Focus your attention on each of the power centers, one at a time, going up your body from the first chakra to the crown. Visualize the color of the portal and see it spinning in a clockwise direction. Then open these centers from the back of your body. You can do this upon waking or resting. I especially enjoy doing this while in the bath, as warm water holds such a conducive quality.

This is a form of activating other types of brains in your body to access additional, and until now, unattainable information. I often find that there are sensations that accompany each of the seven energy centers. The heart can feel like it is softening, opening and or dissolving. Sometimes it feels like a portal that is in itself larger than my body. This can be a somewhat overwhelming feeling but can be a worthwhile journey as it may also lead to rare states of ecstasy and bliss.

Lesson 7
Introspection, Truth and Self-Awareness

Inspiration

"The moment you have in your heart this extraordinary thing called Love and feel the depth, the delight, the ecstasy of it, you will discover that for you, the world is transformed." ~ Jiddu Krishnamurti

Concept

What would your internal landscape look like if you were totally honest with yourself? Forget for the period of working in this exercise your relationship with truth as you have previously understood it. If we cannot be honest with ourselves, it is impossible to be honest with others. Clear your mind of who you want to be and allow yourself to be who you are. What would your world look like if you lived in accordance with your authentic nature? You may stop judging yourself and give yourself permission to accept, settle into and thrive in your idiosyncrasies.

Imagine your life being guided by decisions inspired by Love and kindness towards yourself and others. Give yourself space to know that you don't need to be more than you are now. What is, IS. What if you didn't buy into an illusory agenda or create stories to hold yourself back? Allow yourself to trust and surrender to the idea that you are infinitely held and that your Love is a magnifier, which will inevitably be reciprocated by more Love.

Practice

Who would you be if you acknowledged, "I am awesome?" And, "I'm not nearly as awesome as I can be." Allow space for both to be true.

Make a two-sided list. On one side, list 20 things that make you awesome. Own it! Why do your friends appreciate you? What do you do to make the world a better place? How do you take care of your magnificent body? What hurdles have you overcome? How have you imprinted the world in a way that only your unique being offers? What have you accomplished? How do you make other people feel? Be honest, don't exaggerate, but give yourself the opportunity to celebrate your contributions to this world. Recognize that no one does it quite like you do.

On the other side of the page, list the things that frustrate you about yourself. What are the patterns that keep showing up? What are your "if onlys," the things that you've been telling yourself will make you happy? What are the things that you are ashamed of? What are concepts or feelings that continue to reappear in your relationships?

The fact that both of these aspects of yourself share one page is symbolic that all of these things are simultaneously true. You may find that you hold both the wound and the cure in the same body. For each of your insecurities, you will discover examples in your life that actually disprove the stories that your ego creates to hold you back from your potential. Look for examples of when and where your potential cannot be contained and naturally overcome the boundaries that attempt to hold you back. Your potential has a determination of its own and acknowledging it provides strength. Your body, your experience, the tools and wisdom that you own are simply a container for the work that your highest self, your greatest potential, needs to express in the world.

This exercise is intended to access and utilize the wounded parts of ourselves in service of our potential. This is very fertile ground and brings purpose, compassion and understanding of ourselves, our lineage and the world that has shaped us. The goal is to feel alignment to Source because each of us is a conduit to and in harmony with Love.

Lesson 8
Healing Yourself

Inspiration

My body is an absolutely perfect vessel for me at this time. It is a temple, which I care for and which serves me in every instance. It is the container for my life and provides me the opportunity to experience the beauty and magic of this world. This body is mine alone. It is the only one I have. It has the potential to share with me profound depths of awareness and hold me in my quest for higher understanding.

Concept

As we've found in the previous exercises, it is essential to be receptive to Love. Without being able to absorb and integrate Love, it cannot settle inside of us. As with any force, it must be met. The body is an accumulation of cells working in a brilliant orchestration of movement and cooperation. How would your body feel if you bathed each cell in light? Imagine what it would feel like to care for your whole being by nourishing yourself with Love on a cellular level. This can be a daily practice of bathing all of your cells in universal Love, every single one. Imagine that Love is a force so strong that it actually fills the empty space in each of the atoms currently making up the tissue in your body.

I have a tendency towards empathy, and I noticed when others would tell me about their ailments, I began to feel their sensations in my body. I began to practice surrounding myself in pure light to shield me from taking on others' energy while listening. I would then imagine the essence of pure light filling my body, cleansing each cell with the intention of health, safety and wellness.

Imagine your cells functioning more efficiently, unhindered by unnecessary resistance.

Practice

Allowing the force of Love into your body can begin with a simple scan. In the same way that a laser printer processes each millimeter working through a page, imagine surveying your body from top to bottom. It may start slowly bringing attention to the places that you are holding tension. I usually give the imagined scan some tangible or visual quality such as a light, color, or texture.

Observe your body and fill it with clear light. You may feel like you are dislodging blockages, opening up dark, stagnant space to fill it with spacious light. Once you feel some freedom, play with color by invoking a variety of shades in the rainbow. Each time you scan your body, the light will find less resistance until it flows seamlessly. Try textures like water, sand or honey.

This practice can be done anywhere and at any time. It can take as much or as little time as you need. I now find myself doing this automatically when I am scared or uncomfortable. This practice informs me of what it is that I need to understand about the situation. When something rings true for me, I can feel this as a sensation in my body. As with everything, the more you practice, the more enhanced your awareness becomes.

Lesson 9
You are a Love-Powered Super(s)hero

Inspiration

Healthy am I, Happy am I, Holy am I…

As you repeat this, feel into the essence of it. Dissuade your mind from creating commentary. Allow for an open mind and feel health pervading your being, then happiness, then holiness, then all simultaneously.

Concept

Let us imagine, even if for the time that you are reading this book, Love is source energy. Love is the unifying force that binds us. It is both the question and the answer. It has no beginning and no end. It is where we come from and into which we will return. Let us table our critical mind that questions its source, rather accepting that this powerful force may be the essence from which all religions, mysticism and devotional practices evolved. Imagine that Love is the source of the prism from which these ideas manifested.

Practice

What would it feel like to embody the most divine expression of yourself? To know yourself as a being of pure Love. Who would you be? How would you show up in your life? How would you embody Love in a way that doesn't require restrictions, limitations, biases or stories connected to it? Imagine living a life fueled by pure, unfiltered Love. Take each of these questions and ponder it for five minutes. Give your imagination to it. Allow yourself to be a super(s)hero version of yourself. What would your Love-powered super(s)hero do and say? How would this super-lover act at home, on the street, at work or with friends and family?

Lesson 10
Conscious Communication

Inspiration

I Perceive in Love

I Think in Love

I Speak in Love

I Act in Love

I Work in Love

I Concentrate in Love

I am Mindful in Love

Concept

Communication is critically important because it is how we navigate the world. Buddhism holds the Eight-Fold Path as one of its principal tenets.

The Eight-Fold Path is considered a precept to living one's life in the highest alignment to one's true nature. Although the following aspirations are not necessarily considered to have any specific order, you may find that they build on each other.

I - Right Understanding, II - Right Thought, III - Right Speech, IV - Right Action, V - Right Livelihood, VI - Right Effort, VII - Right Concentration, VIII -Right Mindfulness

Every one of these is worthy of deep contemplation and study. However, for the purpose of attending to conscious communication, I will speak to Right Speech, which is at the center of it all. Each of these tenants can be considered in the context of multiple layers of the internal, external and unseen worlds of our perception. Right Speech, therefore, can influence how we communicate with ourselves and others consciously and unconsciously. Imagine if we genuinely and consistently spoke to ourselves in kindness, with the understanding and acceptance that we may want or expect of others. How can we expect others to treat us with the kindness we deserve if we do not treat ourselves with such kindness? We demonstrate consciously or unconsciously our expectations of others through our internal dialogue. We can change the quality of interactions with others and how others communicate with us through verbal and nonverbal expression.

This is not about being nicer or better. It is about tweaking the quality of your communication with self and others to take responsibility for and influence your understanding, thought, action, livelihood, effort, concentration and mindfulness.

There is a ripple effect as all of these precepts are connected, and we are all connected. The change will ripple through you, then ripple throughout your world.

Practice

Communication is often about needs and desires. Although needs and desires can be quite different, they are connected in this practice to give you the opportunity to address either or both. 1. What do you need or desire from yourself? 2. What do you need or desire from others? What do you need or desire from whom? 3. Can you express your needs and desires? 4. Decipher where each need or desire comes from. How can you feel complete, even if the outcome of your need or desire does not come from outside of yourself? 6. Do you believe that you are worthy of having your needs and desires met?

For the first two questions, write down five answers for each. For the third, give three examples of where you can express your needs and three examples of where you cannot. For the fourth question, go through all your answers and explore where these needs and desires come from and how you could feel satisfied without anyone else's participation. Take as much responsibility for your feelings as you can. Self-truth is your champion. Remember, only you have the answers to your questions, and only you can set yourself free. Now consider the last question.

This exercise is designed to help you unravel some of the patternings that make you think the way you do. Our thinking is deeply ingrained and has served us in the past for innumerable purposes, but does our old thinking, our self-communication, serve our highest good now? Or are there places where it limits our thinking, our relationships and ultimately ourselves? Can we redirect our speech, understanding, thought, action, livelihood, effort, concentration, and mindfulness to be experienced through the honesty of Love?

There are 1,000 words in Arabic for Love.

Lesson 11
Love as a Meditation

Inspiration

You can listen to the following song, "Long Time," Sun by Snatam Kaur from the album *Grace* on YouTube.

May the long time sun shine upon you

All Love surround you

And the pure light within you

Guide your way on

Guide your way on

Sat Nam (truth is my identity)

Concept

Many spiritual traditions use Love as a meditation for the healing of humanity. This Tonglen meditation is designed to connect you in the experience of Love with the world around you.

Pema Chödrön, an American, Tibetan Buddhist nun of the Shambhala tradition, shares this Tonglen meditation. You can find her entire teaching here:

https://youtu.be/QwqlurCvXuM

"On the in-breath, you breathe in whatever particular area, group of people, country, or even one particular person... [Y]ou breathe in with the wish that those human beings or those mistreated animals or whoever it is, that they could be free of that suffering, and you breathe in with the longing to remove their suffering.

And then you send out – just relax out... send enough space so that peoples' hearts and minds feel big enough to live with their discomfort, their fear, their anger or their despair, or their physical or mental anguish. But you can also breathe out for those who have no food and drink. You can breathe out food and drink. For those who are homeless, you can breathe out/send them shelter. For those who are suffering in any way, you can send out safety, comfort.

So, in the in-breath, you breathe in with the wish to take away the suffering and breathe out with the wish to send comfort and happiness to the same people, animals, nations, or whatever it is you decide.

Do this for an individual, or do this for large areas. If you do this with more than one subject in mind, that's fine... breathing in as fully as you can, radiating out as widely as you can."

Practice

Imagine someone else or yourself at another time in your life (childhood, adolescence or a specific moment of trauma) as the focus of your intention. Hold that person in your attention and give that being as much Love as you are capable of offering. Do this without any attachment to any particular outcome. Do this only because you truly desire this person to be held in pure Love. Feel the strength and depth of the Love that you are directing towards your subject. Feel that you are a conduit for Love, that you are giving yourself the chance to both receive and direct Love. Know that you can overcome any judgment that your mind may have. Simply open yourself up to Love, not for yourself, but for the sincere purpose of funneling Love to someone else. There is something very profound about this practice. It allows you to receive, cultivate and generate the pure force of Love while not staying attached to it. It is through you, from you, but not for you. The practice is to overcome any attachment to attaining or maintaining Love, while you get to bathe in the beauty of it. Scientists, faith leaders and philosophers have speculated on the outcome for the other person with varying perspectives.

I did this practice one morning and held my father in love for a long time. As adults, we have become estranged, but I loved him as an innocent child who needed only to Love and be Loved. I poured into him all the Love that I could give to this perfect, pure being. I Loved him without regard to any of his life experiences. I held him in divine Love. I held him in divine Love throughout the different passages of his life, passages through which I avoided associating judgment. I Loved him as an observer, not participating in any reaction, not trying to understand, holding him in the infinite expanse of Love. Eventually, I was Loving the man that currently exists in my life. And I was Loving him so deeply and so profoundly that I realized that there was no separation between us. He had given me my life. I am of him. He gifted me some of his life, allowing me to live mine. I was giving him life through continuing his lineage, giving him life beyond his own. It is this evolutionary dance that has given life to us both.

My father and I spoke on the phone later that day, not about anything unusual. There was no mention of my conscious practice. Still, there was a clear difference in the quality of the connection between us. It may have been my experience, or he may have perceived something different. Either way, I was pleased by the lovely connection.

The intention of this practice is for the person doing the meditation to access the experience of knowing, feeling, being and living in the essence of Love. Once this feeling is experienced, it can be reclaimed again and again with increasing potency. To hold this feeling of universal Love and to walk through our world in it is to possess a powerful mechanism by which we can direct our lives and reflect the light of Love into the lives of others.

Visualize this as a projection into the space in front of you. As you move into this space of Love that you are cultivating for yourself, the experiences that you have in Love-consciousness will color everything that you touch, material and non-material; like the fabled Midas Touch, but with Love rather than gold.

Lesson 12
Unify in Love

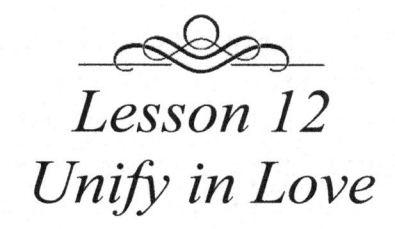

Inspiration

Listen to "Heaven in a Wildflower" on YouTube:

https://youtu.be/k4FOz3T-qBc

"To see a world in a grain of sand,
And heaven in a wildflower,
Hold infinity in the palm of your hand,
And eternity in an hour.
He who binds himself to a joy
Does the winged life destroy:
He who kisses the joy as it flies
Lives in eternity's sunrise."

Music by Bill Douglas, Sung by Ars Nova Singers—from Boulder Creek, Colorado, Lyrics from the poem, "Auguries of Innocence" by William Blake.

Concept

What if we could unify in Love? We wouldn't have to agree on what is right or true, only that we all Love our children and our families, communities and planet. Through this shared force, can we agree to Love this miracle of a planet that provides for us and all of the other sentient beings with whom we share it? What a cohesive force! Where there is Love, there is devotion and commitment. Idealistic, yes! Why not?

"Love is how we are going to create peace on earth."
~ Cameron Powers, founder of Musical Ambassadors of Peace

Do we have the capacity to deeply understand one another? Yes, we do have the extraordinary power to do so if we can interact with each other in a space that does not make one individual right and another wrong. There are too many shades of grey for absolute truth. One infallible truth is that we all have the capacity for Love. Within that capacity, we can see each other as valid human beings with needs, desires, hopes and dreams that may or may not be the same as our own. If we accept our differences with Love, the ultimate outcome would be a reflection of that Love.

I have been acutely interested in studying the root causes of conflict throughout my life, what conflict has to tell us about perception and how conflict can be a catalyst for a deeper understanding of others. Recently I have been focusing my Love on the perpetrators of violence. Yes, victims need Love, support and compassion while violators are in a kind of pain they often cannot even identify.

Soon after returning from the Holy Land, I had an insight coming out of deep meditation of the three Abrahamic Religions being different threads that wove a beautiful tapestry. The tapestry was strengthened and enriched by each of the threads that made the cloth. This insight has allowed me to understand that one string is not stronger than another, but each of the strings is needed as they offer various connections and interpretations of the divine. The tapestry is the world we live in, which we are continually weaving together.

Practice

Imagine this feeling of Love that you have been working on. Think of a time that you have been able to access this feeling and hold it. Direct that feeling to a situation, a region, a people or a cause. Focus. Imagine Love holding and penetrating that which you hold. Imagine the faces of those influenced by your Love. Imagine their hearts softening because you are breathing a breath of Love into their hearts. Stay with this as long as you can. Let the feeling of Love envelop you. Let this Love be both the genesis and the connection. Let it be the essence that connects you with your focus. Hold Love and the object of your focus simultaneously. Let them linger together in this nutritive and healing space.

Lesson 13
How We Live in This Moment is How We Set the Course for the Future

Inspiration

"Life will give you whatever experience is most helpful for the evolution of your consciousness. How do you know this is the experience you need? Because this is the experience you are having at the moment." ~Eckhart Tolle, author of *The Power of Now*

Concept

Everything that you do, say and think in the present are the seeds from which the future will grow. Your present is the beginning of your future. You are constantly manifesting your future in your current actions. Therefore, you have absolute free will to change the course of your life with the thinking and decision making that you subscribe to in each moment. Some people call it cause and effect; some people call it karma.

Think of how far a reputation precedes you. A reputation is the result of those around you, noticing patterns of behavior. No one is perfect, but if you are perceived by those around you to be fair and make thoughtful decisions, you will be perceived as honest and trustworthy. That reputation will ultimately benefit you in your social and professional worlds. So, with each interaction, you get to choose who you want to BE. You get to choose what is important to you, and ultimately, others decide whether to invest or divest from interacting with you based on how you show up in your life.

Of course, many things in our lives are beyond our control. What is within our domain to change is how we perceive these occurrences. A life-changing moment for me was after my daughter died when a therapist was brave enough to tell me that what was perpetuating my suffering was the belief that she shouldn't have died. Because my daughter died of medical negligence six days after her birth, that was very difficult for me to hear and accept. I was so attached to my unwavering belief that she should be alive that I wasn't living in the reality that she was not. I will forever be grateful for this person, for, in that instant, I understood that it was my own thinking that was holding me captive.

Fortunately, I had the capacity to change that and set myself free. I accepted the reality of what WAS, and that gave me the strength to move forward in my life. I couldn't change the past; she was gone. I couldn't bring her back with anything that I thought, felt or believed, but I could begin to live in the present and look into the future without being chained to a past that I could not change.

We can change our perception of reality by changing our perception of what IS reality. Think of the study about poor people who win the lottery and return to poverty after a while. It is about the perception of abundance. Even after having a wealth of money, they intrinsically still consider themselves poor and eventually land back in that state of being. What if you began to believe that you were perfectly cared for and your needs were being met? Hold that to be true and see what happens. This is not magic; it is the surrender of allowing yourself to simply be with what is and easefully live into the world in which you want to participate.

Practice

The future is uncertain. By some estimates, scientists predict that Earth will be uninhabitable by 2050. If we lived in this future possibility, fear could consume us. I did not write that statistic to conjure fear; I wrote it so that we can see that we make decisions in each moment of our lives that have consequences on the future we are creating. We can choose to live in a harmonious, respectful relationship with our planet or not. There are certainly consequences for our current choices, so we must be thoughtful about the choices we make and how we show up for ourselves, each other and the Earth. The NOW is the gateway to the future.

What do you want in the future? How can you activate that in your life right now? Make a list of the things that you want to live into. They can be goals that are long term or short term. Write each one on a separate piece of paper. Let's say, "I want to bring regional neighbors together in

Jordan to celebrate humanity through music, dance and art." Answer the question, what can I do today to launch that into being? Write down your answer under the goal. Tomorrow, ask yourself the same question and write down the answer. Ask yourself the same question each day until the page is full. If this is helpful, continue the practice until it is clear how you need to show up in your life each day and each moment to become the person you see in your future. Eventually, you will not have to write it down; you will have the fortitude in knowing what you need to do in the now to meet your future.

Lesson 14
Intuition and Magnetism Follow Your Flow

Inspiration

"I am _____. I am anchored in my connection to the Spirit that guides me in all ways and at all times. I am anchored in my connection to my Highest Self, who is devoted to my growth and healing in all ways and at all times. I offer myself in the service of the mission that brought me here, and I embrace the healing of all the wounds that have kept me hidden from my Self. I want to know who I am. I anchor in my heart the desire for connection with my truest Self. I anchor compassion for my journey and the journey of others. I anchor commitment to this process and its grace-filled unfoldment. I anchor willingness to explore what lies beneath the habits, behaviors, patterns, attachments, beliefs and energies that have limited me in the past. I ask that all habits, behaviors, patterns, attachments, beliefs and energies that no longer serve me to be gently and gracefully released at this time. I ask that the space left behind to be filled with Love, seeping into and filling every cell of my body, my chakras and my energy field. I breathe deeply and receive this

Love. I breathe deeply and receive this Love again and again and again." ~Author unknown

Concept

What would it feel like to stay a little longer, to take a different path or give an unknown person a big, authentic, radiant smile for no reason? What would it feel like to push your boundaries, the limitations that keep you held back from the rest of the world? Visualize how it would be to slow down and walk through life with an open heart as your guide. What would the sensation be like to deeply feel your experiences? Imagine what it would be like to take a deep breath and hold a place of unknowing for a moment before making a decision in order to see if a different kind of knowing shows up. Think about walking more slowly and paying more attention to where you are and what is happening all around you. It has always been fascinating to me when I notice the things that I have consistently overlooked.

My very best friend used to hug me longer than I did. It didn't make me uncomfortable. It was always a delight to be in her embrace, but it made me recognize that I pulled out of a perfectly good embrace before it was finished. I began to surrender into her embrace longer and longer until my heart felt calm and content in the moment and oh so satisfied afterward. This is a small example of what an investigation into surrender looks like but a good place to start. Let yourself stay in a hug a bit longer, even for just an extended moment, to see if there is something more there that you have been missing. Can you return someone's gaze for a moment longer, or at all? Why does this feel challenging? Can you let your awkwardness, expectation or self-consciousness dissolve? Can you stay present long enough to feel it; to feel the connection with another person?

How are you showing up to your life's experiences? When a new experience shows up, see if there is an opportunity for change inside of it. If you are blocked by traffic, maybe there is something in the adjoining neighborhood that has value for you. Consider the saying, "God never shuts one door without opening another one."

In my own life, when I am able to stay present, I can welcome adversity, knowing that something wasn't right for me, and I must be patient to find the way forward. When I am able to embrace change with this perspective, I am always grateful for the outcome because it is inevitably better than the previous situation. I know this teeters on faith-based belief. I used to shy away from the very idea of faith, but the funny thing is that the more faith I have in things turning out beautifully, the more they do. I've had to confront the fact that there is some type of reciprocal force with faith - faith in universal flow.

Practice

When new experiences arise, see how much you can show up to fully meet them. Sink in. Be present. How much can you embrace life? Welcome what is. Can you stay present enough to truly be with a person in the moments that you share? Can you do so without anticipation of the next moments that follow? By consciously staying in the present moment, you can change the outcome of the next moment. Experiment and see what happens. Gather information through experience and investigation. Doing so will make you stronger, clearer and more confident. See what it feels like to temporarily suspend that which only contains you and restrains you, awkwardness, expectation, self-consciousness. Give into a hug, show up in it, don't be in the next moment, be in the present one with each person or experience. Slow down. Let your heart be your guide.

I once taught Palestinian children ecstatic dance in various refugee camps in the West Bank. I acknowledged that there was little that I could do to change the circumstances of their lives, but I could guide them to feel freedom within their own bodies.

Lesson 15
Love Is So Much More Than Attraction

Inspiration

I love you, all of you

Your faults and mistakes

Your past and potential

Your power and insecurities

I love the way you make me feel when there is light in your eyes

and you look at me as though I materialized through magic

You are the one that I choose, I choose all of you

Even the parts that you haven't shown me yet

Even the person you are in your most trying days

I will love you when you forget to love yourself

I will love you full and strong and loyal and tough

With the determination to love you into your best

Concept

We all live in bodies, and sex can complicate the idea of Love. For some, it's easier to Love someone that they are attracted to. For others, it is easier to Love outside of attraction, a place where there is no hidden agenda, expectations or attachment to the future. Unfortunately, attraction can lead to feeling reserved and self-conscious, which is not a place that Love flows freely.

When attraction is present, it is natural to wonder if another reciprocates your feelings. So, if Love is ultimately the goal in coupling, the challenge is to table attraction long enough to Love someone as a human being without the attraction to a human body. What if initiating a connection with someone you are attracted to started with an open heart rather than one scared of possible misperception? What if it doesn't matter if this Love and attraction have a future? Imagine Love being expressed in its essence for the sake of experiencing the purity of it.

What if you filled up someone else's heart and were capable of being filled by theirs, beyond attraction? Allow yourself to visualize how it would feel to approach a relative, a neighbor, a colleague or a platonic friend with an open heart? Now imagine that same ease with someone you are attracted to. Any two people can Love each other, whereas not all people are attracted to each other. What a shame it is to ever hold back on giving Love abundantly. Our world is a container holding all of us who simultaneously need Love and have an abundance of Love to give. Can we meet each other with our hearts courageously open?

I relished a story a friend once shared with me about her confronting her attraction. She told the subject of her adoration, "I have a crush on you, so if I act weird around you, that's why." She said it, as a matter of fact, not needing a response. The receiver was grateful for the compliment, and it became something that they laughed about. Then their tension wasn't weird anymore, and that was the beginning of their story.

I Love that story because she brushed her ego and fear aside and declared her truth. She said it without a charge. The statement was disarming, authentic and honest, allowing the receiver to see her as having those traits.

Love certainly can be, and often is, a conduit to sex, but it is also a force that can deepen connection without physical intimacy. Any two people can Love each other if they are willing to see each other's innate self.

Practice

Write a Love poem to your dearest beloved. Whether you know that person or not. Whether you can even imagine this person or not. If you exist, your equal opposite also exists. Write your letter with total abandon. Express exactly how much you love this person and why. Express the depth of your Love and all that you are capable of giving. Allow yourself to surrender to the devotion of Love. Write your devotion as an invitation to the beloved whom you have not yet met.

Do it, and don't read the next part until you do!

Now read this poem to yourself because it is for you!

This represents how much Love you have to give as well as how much Love you are capable of receiving.

Lesson 16
Letting Go

Inspiration

"I've decided to be happy
I've decided to be glad
I've decided to be grateful
For all I ever had
I've decided to let go
Of all this pain tonight
I've decided to let go
Of all these demons inside
I know...I am blessed
I know...all I ever wanted was this
I know...I don't need more
I've got... what I came for
I've decided to be open
To that little voice inside
Telling me I'm beautiful
It's okay to be alive

I've decided to be kinder

To myself when I feel sad

I've decided to be grateful

For all I ever had."

~ Kinder by Copper Wimmin

https://youtu.be/P9PX31Ioh_c

Concept

If you hold onto sand too firmly, you will squeeze it out of your grip.

There is no greater release than to surrender something to Love. To let something fall away with grace and ease can be the greatest gift one can give themselves. To allow that which no longer serves you to take a new form or dissipate is a gift. If there was once Love, tuck that into your heart's treasure box and let the rest go. Poof! Like the wind spreading dandelion seeds. If it no longer serves your highest alignment, if it doesn't resonate with your highest frequency, release it. Say thank you and goodbye.

It took two and a half years of separation before my ex-husband and I finalized our divorce. I couldn't explain why we had remained separated for so long. We had no intention of being a couple again, but we weren't ready to let go. One day at *A Course in Miracles*, I had a major revelation. I realized that we had stayed together all this time because we hadn't yet reached the capacity of understanding Love enough to part ways in pure Love. I realized that our lesson was to part in the wholeness of

Love. Once I understood, I knew that it was time, and we are now dear friends and supportive co-parents. We needed each of the experiences that we shared, the good, the bad and the ugly, in order to understand more deeply what Love is even as it changed shape. Love is passion, communication, support, understanding as well as something far greater than the sum of all of these.

Each of our experiences is a prop in our personal Love stories. Each obstacle on one's own journey is unique, but the essence of the destination is the same. It is Love that supports and binds all things. Love is a practice. It is not one of sacrifice; it is one of bounty. If you are not feeling bountiful, use Love as a practice to shift your situation into one that is fulfilling and satisfying.

Old models of relating, such as codependence, are failing while the evolution of conscious, communicative connection is providing space for Love to exist in more supportive and sustainable ways. Relationships are being reorganized to fit into our collective experiences of higher consciousness.

If there was once Love, it would live on in some fashion. It may shift into something else: forgiveness, understanding, compassion, even hatred. Hatred is simply the fierceness of Love upside down, misunderstood and misaligned.

Practice

Think of the things that are not serving you in your life at this time, such as influences in your life, attitudes, conditioning, perceptions, people, situations, etc. To each say, "Thank you. You may have once served me, but you are no longer needed." It is important to acknowledge the understandings that each of life's experiences has provided for you. We would not be the same people if it weren't for the collage of experiences that have shaped us, and in reflection, we can be grateful for each of them.

As with all of the other exercises and practices, this process will assist you in finding relief from the pressure of your current burdens and permit you to go back in time and clean out some of the old emotional junk that you have been hoarding. Without needing to literally approach the conversation, you can symbolically thank your parents or other influencers for some of the beliefs that they instilled in you that no longer resonate. Give them back without judgement saying, "Thank you, this no longer serves me, you can have it back."

"I am not what happened to me, I am what I choose to become." ~ Carl Jung

Lesson 17
Forgiveness

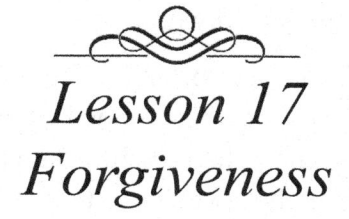

Inspiration

See through the eyes of the Divine

You are its most beloved

You are innocent

Each of the creatures of this earth is a representation of the Divine

Know that you are perfectly whole and loved by Source as you are in this moment

And others are also perfectly whole and loved by Source as they are in this moment

Concept

As previously mentioned, my first daughter Azaria was six days old when she died as a result of a series of mistakes made by my birth practitioner during a long labor. It was a shattering way to enter parenthood. My body was also quite wounded, and I was lucky to eventually be able to carry and birth my second daughter Izabela. I was wholly shattered, devastated beyond imagination. It felt like I was disembodied in galactic proportions. There are so many stages of grief that I experienced, but the one that was the most intense was my rage.

I was in graduate school at the time studying conflict in the Middle East, and that seemed tame to the battles terrorizing my psyche. There were a number of instances that brought me to the awareness that it was I that was perpetuating my suffering. I assumed that the woman who caused my daughter's death was probably experiencing her own suffering. My suffering wasn't making her suffer more. Her suffering didn't make my suffering less. I realized that it wasn't until I disassociated with this woman, uncrossed our paths and let her out of my life, would I be free. It was my decision. The only way she remained in my life was by me sustaining her presence there.

One day the pain was just too great. I had to do something, so I let her go. I didn't want her in my life any longer. I didn't want to torture myself any further. I was exhausted. It took me a few more years to actually forgive her, but I did. I no longer needed to hold on to the pain. What happened, happened. It happened to both of us. It happened to all of us. Making her wrong was not going to bring my daughter back. The only thing that was going to save me from myself was forgiving her. Because my hate was destroying me, I forgave her and allowed the pain she had caused me to evaporate. It no longer had control over me. I gained my life back, and she no longer lingers in my consciousness.

It was then that I allowed joy to seep in, then happiness, and eventually Love. To feel Love is the greatest gift one can give and receive. When our hearts are filled with darkness, there is no space for light. It is up to us to choose what we want to fill our hearts and minds with. It is what we fill ourselves with, which is then reflected back to us. To forgive is to take our power back. It is taking responsibility for our feelings, torment and suffering. Forgiveness has nothing to do with what exists outside of us. It is our freedom alone. If something no longer bothers you, think of how much space, clarity, energy and freedom you have. Your nemesis no longer controls you because you no longer give up your power. You are the commander of your perception.

Practice

Imagine that the essence of pure Love is looking down upon you and Loving you, unconditionally. When I imagine this, I perceive pure Love as an angel that embodies motherly tenderness and a gentle smile of wisdom. Although it is understandably difficult to fathom Source with our inherently limited capacity for grasping the boundless and infinite, imagine the presence of pure Love holding you in total, divine acceptance. Imagine Source seeing all of your inner workings, holding you and appreciating you as nothing less than total perfection. Let yourself surrender to the glory of knowing that regardless of your faults, you are absolute perfection.

Remember and repeat, "I am whole, I am pure, I am innocent. I am exactly who and where I am supposed to be." Let Love in and with it, allow yourself to feel Love, to bathe in it and be nourished by it. Let Love gently wash away your judgements of yourself. Allow yourself to be seen and appreciated as the magnificent being that you are.

Imagine this angelic Love as all-encompassing, softly soothing you into an understanding of how much you are loved. Imagine this Source is the essence of a compassionate mother who sees only your goodness and holds you in that knowing. For her, there is no need for judgement. She can only see your goodness. She only knows Love. Anything other than Love that you feel at this time is an illusion, a story to keep you separated from pure Love. In this moment, relinquish this story to be fully receptive to Love. This bounty of Love has the potential to heal past wounds as you realize they no longer serve you. Only your own courage in receiving this unconditional Love serves you in this moment. It is your openness and vulnerability that allows the Love in. Know that this Source is always there loving you. It is up to you to accept when, where and to what capacity you are able to access this Love and let it transform you.

I recently had a conflict with a friend. When we met to talk about it, we gave each other a big hug, and I could feel our hearts connecting. We didn't even need to talk about our problem. It became comically insignificant in the arch of the Love that we shared in reuniting in Love.

Lesson 18
Non-Judgement

Inspiration

I allow all things to be as they are

I bless all things with Love

Concept

When I think about judgement, I think about polarity, that which differentiates us. It is our ego trying to elevate us above another. Judgement is a lack of understanding, the opposite of curiosity. It is different than discernment, which is an internal compass that directs us towards our true personal north. Judgement is a way for us to escape a shared reality; to exclude ourselves from coexistence. It separates us by perpetuating a belief that we are better or more righteous than others. Judgement alienates us from a world of possibilities that we may not even be aware of.

I recently heard the Taoist story of a man who lost his horse. When his neighbors came to him and said, "What bad luck," the man said, "Perhaps." The next day the horse came back with seven wild horses, and his neighbors came to him and said, "What good luck." And the man said, "Perhaps." The next day his son was training one of the wild horses, fell and broke his leg. His neighbors came to him and said, "What bad luck," and he said, "Perhaps." The next day the army came to conscript men for war but refused the man's son because of his broken leg. His neighbors came to him and said, "What good luck," and he said, "Perhaps."

Imagine the lack of anxiety this man attained in suspending his judgement. This story demonstrates that the father had no control over external events that dictated his life, only his attachment to them.

Consider what it could be like to be open-minded and open-hearted enough to fully appreciate that there may be truth in things that we personally do not understand.

Consider what could change in your perception and relationships if you explored the places within you where your internal voice of judgement exists.

Our judgement perpetuates that which we dislike. Imagine if you un-tie yourself from the bonds of your unhappiness by letting go of judgement.

By not engaging your mind with beliefs of what should and should not be, you let the world be as it is. You have the capacity to redirect your focus from what you dislike in order to make space for what you want to welcome. Making more space in your mind for the world that you want to see diminishes that which you disapprove of.

Mahatma Gandhi, the great practitioner of non-violence, would simply advocate for non-participation in that which we cannot condone. Our participation perpetuates the problem. Perhaps the most profound way to disarm and invalidate something is to stop participating in it.

I hold considerable judgement towards violence, greed and intolerance. The more I dismantle these qualities from my scope of perception, the more I disengage in their generation and perpetuation. The less I hold these ideas of fear and aggression, the more space I have for Love. Love that I can use to rise above violence, greed and intolerance.

When I imagine a peaceful world, I see the suspension of judgement as a critical component. Restorative Justice asks, when is someone wrong and when is that person misunderstood? What if, by making someone wrong, they become a perpetrator? What if we began to question the reasons for our internal battles, asking, where are we the perpetrators of our thoughts?

Practice

Think of a situation that disturbs you. Write down five or more things that upset you about it. In order to change these things, wouldn't it be best to start in an arena where you have a modicum of control, your own heart and mind? There is always such a thing as a tipping point, and it is our shared consciousness that shapes the change. The individual mind of each one of us directs the malleability of this tipping point. Therefore, we collectively dictate the thinking that shapes our world. We invest in the world's belief systems through the ideas and thinking that we buy into. Where are we perpetuating the things that we hold to be most vile?

I'm going to do this with you.

I see a lot of judgement, violence, fear and shame perpetuated from religious extremism.

1. Hiding behind religious absolutism negates the multitude of other perspectives that exist in the world.
2. Extremists can be dishonest about the faith, tweaking it to satisfy their worldview.
3. Religious extremism is a way to control populations by dissuading them from asking questions.
4. Extremism negates considering the similarities of other faith practices and can lead to intolerance.
5. Leaders of religious extremist groups often manipulate their followers through fear and reward.

So, in looking at these beliefs that I have listed as most vile to me, it does not seem as though I have much in common with the ideas. Still, because I share the same planet with these movements, I am living within the intricate web of its existence.

How have I contributed to the existence of that which I find most vile, and how can I be a remedy for it? Where am I the cause and the solution? The above five statements invite me to ponder the following questions.

1. Where do I hide behind absolutism? How do I negate the multitude of perspectives that exist in the world?
2. When am I dishonest with myself, tweaking something to satisfy my worldview?

3. Is there a way that I try to control a preexisting narrative by dissuading myself from asking questions and learning more?
4. Where in my life am I intolerant?
5. Have I fallen victim to being manipulated by fear and reward? Have I perpetrated manipulation through fear and reward?

Gandhi did not remove the British Empire out of the whole of India with hatred in his mind, weapons in his hands or the need for domination in his heart. He knew that combative thoughts could only lead to greater suffering. He accomplished his mission with prayer in his mind, a loom in his hands and Love in his heart. He was active in countering that which he saw as morally wrong. He succeeded not by participating in the oppression of others but by creating a model for citizens to actively disengage in a suppressive system.

I highly recommend the Tom Shadyac documentary, I AM.

Lesson 19
Beauty

Inspiration

Beauty is my beloved, my guide and my direction
It is the stream through which I swim
Beauty shines through my eyes to touch all that I see
It is the lens of my perception
Beauty becomes the droplets of joy that infuse my reality
It inspires gratitude, fulfillment, LOVE

Concept

What is the feeling that beauty brings you? What happens in your imagination when you embrace beauty in its purest form without judgement? It could be a magical sunset dipping into the horizon, an awe-inspiring, majestic mountain, the innocence of a child or the sight of a beloved. Beauty exists in all things if we attune our vision to it.

Practice

Visualize something that conjures the idea of pure beauty. Hold your vision inside of your heart for the length of a breath. Breathe it in, hold it, feel it, then exhale. How did it feel to hold beauty inside of your body? Peaceful? Fulfilling? You may be brought to the precipice of tears of joy. This is the sensation of Love.

See if you can do it again for more than one breath. See if you can breathe in that beautiful feeling and hold it gently. Bathe in the sensation of beauty. Let it fill the entirety of you.

This practice is to train your brain to see through the lens of beauty. You can decide to shift your vision in a way that allows more beauty into your awareness. What would your life look like if you lived in a world of beauty? Could you see more color, feel more texture, notice more depth? What more could we perceive? Who would you be? How would you feel walking through that world? Joyous? Delighted? Intrigued?

Lesson 20
Looking into the Shadows

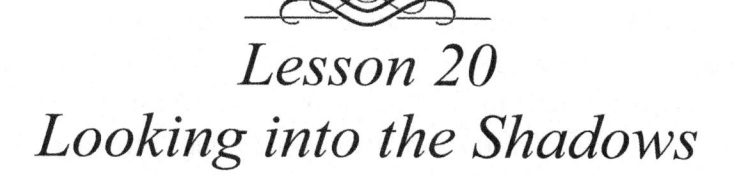

Inspiration

The March 11, 2016 TED Radio Hour podcast named What We Fear features a talk by Karen Thompson Walker titled "What's the Difference Between Rational and Irrational Fears?" It's worth a listen.

https://www.npr.org/programs/ted-radio-hour/archive?date=2016-03-25&eid=384949524

Concept

The conversation titled, *What We Fear*, linked above, discusses fear as a tool for us to better understand who we really are. If we can honestly assess our fears, they can be a guide or storyteller about what resides in our conscious or unconscious minds. I found this to be so fascinating because I thought that I was a relatively fearless person. However, when I began to shine a light on what fear means to me, I was surprised to find out how much was there. None of my fears are crippling, but by bringing awareness to them, I saw how fear directs my choices and my perceptions. I began to play with my fear, asking myself, what would actually happen if my fears manifested?

Science tells us that we are hardwired to feel fear as a protectant against danger, and I cannot dispute that. Thankfully, we have instincts that serve our self-preservation. However, what about all the rest of those unneeded fears? Which of our fears serve self-preservation and which serve as self-limitations? As I began to weed this out for myself, I confronted many of the self-limiting beliefs that I didn't realize I held. As I unpacked these various beliefs, I realized that there is nothing more damaging to myself than my own consciousness. I began wondering if I was living in a cage of consciousness that I had constructed with the limits I had created for myself.

When I came to terms with the answer to my question, it reminded me of the saying, "You can hurt my body but cannot touch my soul." I do not wish harm to my body and deeply appreciate that it works as well as it does. However, nothing less than death would make me return to living in a cage of fear.

The release of fear is one of the most potent experiences of my life. I realize that I am timeless, that my body does not dictate my presence or experience - my consciousness does. Each of us will eventually leave our bodies, that is certain. So, to say yes to life and experience it without unneeded fear is freedom.

Say, for instance, you are afraid of spiders. That's valid; many people are. You may be familiar with the word arachnophobe. I am not asking you to go inside of the fear or re-traumatize yourself. You should only look at this from a logical perspective. Acknowledge your fear and ask yourself if it serves you at this time. I am not suggesting that you Love spiders. What I am saying is that rerouting your fear will make space for Love in various parts of your consciousness to blossom in different areas of your life.

Imagine yourself backpacking the Continental Divide Trail in the Rocky Mountains, and with every step, your backpack seems to be getting heavier. Ask yourself what is weighing you down and what you are willing to discard to lighten your load. Imagine how you will be able to move more quickly and smoothly, with more ease and less tension without that extra weight. Metaphorically, the space that you are creating by discarding your fears (baggage) will make way for the goodness (freedom) that you choose to ingest.

Practice

Ask yourself: What am I afraid of? Is that a rational fear? Where did it come from? What does that fear tell me about myself?

As you begin to peel back the layers of that fear, what do you find? How does that fear serve you? Why do you continue to harbor this fear? Imagine what it would look like if this fear had a physical expression. Find where it resides in your body. Does it have a shape, a color or a texture? Is it solid or malleable? Play with it. Can you move it outside of yourself or farther away? Can you change the consistency, texture, color or shape? Can you dissolve it or find it a new home?

What would the quality of your life feel like without carrying the weight of that fear? Now, for just for a moment, replace that fear with something else. You know what I'm going to say – Love! How does that feel?

If your fear is a storyteller that can provide insight into your personal narrative, ask yourself, what if I relinquish knowing the outcome of the story that is perpetuated by fear? Make space to create a new outcome. For instance, your fear tells you that a specific cause is associated with a certain effect, and you believe that will continue to be the case. These assumptions may be worth investigating. When you come to a fork in the road and recognize that you are following the path of fear, you can consciously choose to redirect neurological pathways to make new associations for a different thought rather than perpetuating the ones that you have already experienced.

If death is the worst thing that can happen to us, consider the meaning life could have if we made peace with our eventual death. By acknowledging the inevitability of our death, we can live fully and contently until our last moments on earth, rather than living with a fear of the inescapable. What if we were the navigators of our lives and the directors of our own story? Consider what life would be like if fear no longer had power over us and our minds were free and available to more enjoyable possibilities.

Take on one fear at a time. Don't tackle more than one per day. Let your mind rest in sleep before you choose to investigate another pattern.

Lesson 21
Love is Universal Consciousness

Inspiration

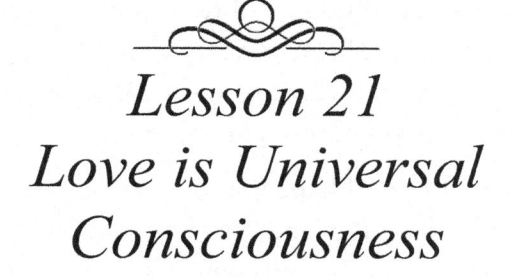

"Love is patient. Love is kind. Love is not jealous; it does not brag. It is not arrogant and does not act unbecomingly. Love does not seek its own. It is not provoked, does not take into account a wrong suffered, does not rejoice in unrighteousness, but rejoices with the truth. Love bears all things, believes all things, hopes all things, endures all things. Love never fails…But now faith, hope, Love, abide these three; but the greatest of these is Love." 1 Corinthians 13: 4-8

Concept

We are born of universal Love. Our deepest longing is to be reunited with this infinite Love through the unique gifts, talents and assets we hold. We can change the world with the impact of Love, and what better time to start than now.

I have always been interested in politics, staying attuned to the news of current events that shape our reality.

I am curious about how ego shapes power and how power shapes human evolution. Politics can be seen as an expression of our collective fears and desires. There is currently an enormous shift in consciousness towards the progressive evolution of thought and action.

All over the world, people are engaged in the most outstanding, innovative and inspirational efforts for the betterment of humanity. We can also see a tremendous amount of suffering, fear, greed and hatred. People from every profession and perspective are challenging outdated paradigms and creating new systems in extraordinary ways.

Hierarchical power structures crumble as humanity awakens to the inability of those structures to serve burgeoning cooperative societies.

It is easy to see someone else's hatred, but it is hard for a person to see his or her own. Hatred is an addiction that feeds itself with more hatred. And that hatred holds a disdain for tolerance as that is its antithesis, the undermining factor that discredits hatred.

So, this work, to recognize and cultivate the power of Love, is critically important to the world we share. It is revolutionary and, in fact, evolutionary. It takes deep courage, the patience of a warrior, and the willingness to think and act as a visionary. It is the power of Love and cooperation that will perpetuate the health and well-being of civilization and the planet that sustains us.

June Jordan's quote, "We are the ones we have been waiting for," reminds me that each generation is perfectly prepared for the work of their time. Each generation blossoms to relieve the previous one of its outdated thinking. Those who wish to perpetuate a system of oppression, intolerance, separation, domination, fear and greed are key players who challenge us to be better, more tolerant, inclusive, inspired, Loving individuals. Every generation is tasked with doing the work of rising up together in creating a cooperative world. Each of us has the opportunity to transform the way we think and live; to live our unique talents and gifts is to embrace life with joy. We can reshape our global society through kindness and tolerance.

Practice

I invite you to use the experience of Love to change your life. What would it feel like to know that everything is in perfect order; to know that you are going to be ok? What if you looked forward to each new day as though it were a special package for you to unwrap? A package that offers you a new opportunity to create something that didn't exist the previous day. What if you welcomed your life with enthusiasm and cherished each moment?

What if you no longer let the little things nag at you? This is not to suggest that you become numb or dispassionate. You will likely find that you feel things more intensely, sadness as well as joy. There cannot be one without the other. Imagine that you just let your feelings, thoughts and beliefs BE without holding onto them or scrutinizing them. Simply allow them to be.

This allows a presence that can be filled with Love. Imagine basking in it when you are driving in traffic, in the line at the grocery store, when preparing for a presentation or a difficult conversation. Try to align yourself as much as you can to Love so that you become a conduit for it.

I am not asking you to abandon all the stories, insights and opinions that you have accumulated in your life. You will always inherently be the same person you have always been, only now with a very compelling compass that guides your words and understanding.

Love is universal. All people can understand what Love is because we can all feel it. Even if we didn't understand anything else about one another, we could connect with another person's culture and society by holding the awareness that we all have the capacity to Love.

Through Love, we can know each other without knowing the other's language, history, faith, race, gender or sexual orientation. We all have hearts and are capable of accessing an enormous capacity to feel. Someday we will recognize that our deep emotional capacity is, in fact, our superpower. The more we attune to Love, the more we will embody an intelligence much greater than we currently understand.

Religion provides a construct to help people understand the infinite power of Love. Religion and faith are pathways to develop relationships with the Divine, which is ultimately Love. It is Love that the saints, buddhas, gurus, seers, prophets, magis, and bodhisattvas have attained: a total understanding of the universal force, Love.

Lesson 22
100 Monkeys

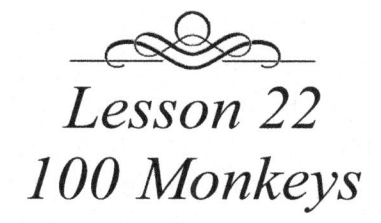

Inspiration

Love is my practice

Love is my devotion

Love is all-consuming

Love is the light, the way and the path

Love is the question and the answer

Love is inside us and all around us

It is simultaneously fueled by us and nourishes us

I am Love, you are Love, we are united in Love

Concept

If we wish to believe that we are all united, that we are pieces of a greater whole, that we can feel each other's pain and bliss, then we accept the inevitability that we influence each other through our thoughts and actions. Some understand this as compassion, empathy or shared consciousness. What if we could influence each other through the radiance, vibration and resonance that we carry?

Early in my self-discovery, a Buddhist friend told me that we are all connected, and if one of us suffers, we all suffer. This has stayed with me throughout my life as it reminds me that we are only as strong as the meek among us. We are not free unless we are all liberated. We suffer if sufferings exist because we are inherently connected. As each of us uncovers our enlightened selves, we enlighten the rest of humanity with our discovery. We are a unit, a network of inter-related, inter-connected beings, that influences each other with our thoughts and actions. Each of us will find the pull and power of synchronicity in different ways and for different reasons. Each in our own time, expression and capacity.

Practice

Upon returning from my first trip to Palestine, I noticed a distinct reaction from a number of people when I spoke about my trip. At times I could feel the quality of interaction change. It was clear that the perception of this region of the world was edgy and uncomfortable for some people.

I share this as it is my hope that if there is a specific cue you find yourself avoiding, try to meet it with curiosity. Ask yourself what your edges are around politics, peace, shared consciousness and the evolution of the human race as a collective entity.

Finding curiosity around our blocks will better inform us individually and collectively about who we are, what we are willing to stand for and how we can show up as change-makers in our lives and in the world. Please know that this comes from a sincere desire for furthering an evolved, united, collective by dismantling judgement, preconceived notions of others and the assumptions that divide us.

I went with a friend to the introduction to the Landmark Forum, and the speaker made a diagram of all the things that we know, the things we don't know, and the things we don't know that we don't know. The latter was by far the largest space. When we ask ourselves the questions posed in this book, we are opening up space in our perception for knowing the things that we didn't previously know that we didn't know. Through this process, we are raising our individual and collective awareness.

I ask you to begin to track the moments when your body tenses, when you stop listening in order to insert your perspective, when you suddenly feel tired or distracted. Begin to let these be points of entry into your inquiry about what lies beyond the moment when you shut down. There will be valuable information for you there.

Lesson 23
Gratitude

Inspiration

Thanks to Source for the sun, the sky, the moon, the wind and clouds, the birds and the stars, for the infinite vastness of space and possibility.

Thanks to our shared home, Earth, for its bounty, diversity, landscapes, all that we eat and drink, flora and fauna, for that which we see, taste, touch, smell and hear. Thanks to the unknown for the mysterious, untouchable curiosities and for all that we can perceive, imagine, believe, share and create. Thanks for the breath of life, the sorrow of death and all of the moments in between. Let us offer a deep bow of gratitude for the grace of knowledge, boundless awe of wonder, wisdom, innocence and for the enveloping impact of Love.

Concept

Gratitude has been a guiding practice that has shaped my life far beyond any explanation I can provide. It began with small things. The day after my daughter Azaria died, I was bewildered by the beauty of the pattern that cream made in my coffee. I was grateful for the Love that existed in my life at the time. Over the years, I made a dedicated effort to acknowledge all of the goodness that has appeared in my life, even if it was fleeting and seemingly inconsequential. I consistently made an effort to notice beauty and kindness, luck and synchronicity. The more I focused on the goodness, the more I noticed it appeared. The more it showed up, the more grateful and so on until I noticed that gratitude is a reciprocal force. Like magnetism, gratitude is a gravitational force strengthening that for which you are grateful.

Gratitude can be as simple as an acknowledgment, taking only a millisecond. It can mingle amongst the millions of thoughts that you have throughout your day. There is nothing about gratitude that is depleting or takes time away from other thoughts or actions. It is simply the act of acknowledging the goodness in your life. Acknowledging this moment, the one right now, when you are precisely where you are supposed to be, is an expression of appreciation.

Every time I become aware of this beautiful place that I live, a place of Love, I am consumed by wonderment at how blessed I am. Sometimes I am overwhelmed with gratitude because I see clearly the miracle of life. I live in such deep gratitude that I have even become grateful for the lessons learned from the experience of losing my daughter. Don't get me wrong, I wish I were mothering her living body; although this is not the reality, I feel blessed that I am among the circle of mothers who share an umbilical cord to an angel baby. The experience of loss opened me up in a way that I could not have comprehended before she lived and died. My experience of life is much more profound, having endured her death. And my experience of her continues to evolve in ways that will always be a mystery to me. These are gifts for which I am grateful.

Practice

Think of the greatest asset that you have in your life now, in this instant. It can be a healthy body, the fact that you are alive, have food to eat, have clean air to breathe, a special person in your life, have acquired the education to read this book or the ability to live in a safe environment. That for which you choose to be grateful can be simple or complex. It really doesn't matter where you start because this is just the beginning of an entirely new perception of your life.

Hold this thing or idea that you are grateful for in your mind. Hold it in Loving appreciation. Recognize how blessed you are to have this in your life. Avoid comparing your experience with anyone else's. You will never fully understand another's experience, so to judge yours against another's is only an exercise in futility. This is your life; only you can fully experience it. This is your truth and what you have to build upon.

Hold this gratitude in your mind and see if you can open your heart with it. Feel the gratitude. Stay with this as long as you can. Hold it until you can feel this quality expanding throughout your mind and body!

The practice is to tap into this feeling as often as possible. It may begin with a conscious effort once a day, or it may be fluid and intuitive. Again, it doesn't matter how the process shows up for you as long as you are able to access the feeling. The goal is to expand gratitude into all aspects of your life. It is like a switch; once you turn it on, you may find that there are more and more things that are worthy of your appreciation. Once you can access the feeling of gratitude, take time to be with the sensation. Experiment with how often you can conjure the feeling of gratitude. See if you can surprise yourself. You have nothing to lose.

Lesson 24
Active Love Affects Our Consciousness, Communities and Planet

Inspiration

My heart is mine, my heart is yours, my heart permeates and absorbs all that exists; it is my barometer of consciousness, my compass of integrity. It guides me towards my divinity and destiny. My heart, aligned with the noble purpose of others, has the strength to heal the world.

Concept

What happens when we get curious? And truly listen? What happens when we check our judgements at the door and replace them with curiosity? What would happen if you could temporarily hold a space for yourself to not immediately be right, but instead, find out if there is something another person is expressing that you have not yet been able to understand? Get curious until you have a greater understanding of what the other person is expressing.

Allow yourself to fully consider what others are saying, even if it conflicts with your own world view. Find out how they came to their conclusion or perspective.

We can heal ourselves and ease our own rigidity by considering that we do not hold absolute truth. Try to honor an opposing opinion by acknowledging that even the most vile of perspectives (according to you) is coming from someone's truth.

We can learn something new and arrive closer to the center of truth by acknowledging that we may not possess absolute truth but may only hold a certain perspective of it. Practice superimposing your judgement with curiosity. Ask questions. Suspend your need to be right and honestly listen to the answers to the questions you ask.

We all have our opinions, and ultimately no two people will ever see the world through the exact same lens. Acknowledging our differences helps us understand what is important to us. Conflict shapes us. An open mind can help us construct our truth more clearly. If we stay curious inside of conflict, it can be a prism of insight.

For instance, having studied the wounding of the Middle East over the last 20 years, I learned that regardless of how we perceive conflict from the comfort of our homes, we often fail to consider the basic truth that indigenous people want foreign powers out of their land.

A common argument a gun owner will give about owning a weapon often goes something like this. "If someone comes into my home, I have the right to protect myself and my family." So why can't we, as a community of nations, understand that no one likes people coming into their homes, communities or land? If we stopped to see that the micro and the macro in these examples share a common experience of people not wanting to have their homes invaded by outsiders, we might be able to recognize a common human experience.

If we are too attached to being righteous about our actions, we will never be able to grow in our understanding. It is the understanding of the shared human experience that drives the evolution of consciousness. By collaborating in the shared experiences of being human, we will eventually stop tolerating or enabling the killing of other humans.

Practice

Please see the Ted Radio Hour - Dialogue and Exchange

https://www.npr.org/programs/ted-radio-hour/558307433

This is a practice that each of us can employ in our daily lives. To begin, notice when judgement arises. If there is another person with whom that judgement is associated, ask a question to clarify something that you may not understand. Start small, with less charged topics and simple language. Refrain from creating your own answer to what you are hearing; make space in your mind to listen deeply. Employ statements like, "I don't fully understand" or "Say more about that." Remember, this is not about you changing someone else's mind or even about changing your own mind. This is simply about understanding where the liminal space is in between what you currently understand and gathering information that you do not yet have.

If you allow yourself to listen carefully, you may hear something that you had not expected. This is not an exercise intended to change your beliefs on any specific topic; it is an exercise designed to ease the rigidity and attachment to being right. This is an experiment to find out if each of us can acknowledge that two or more truths can exist simultaneously. When we recognize that there may not be any one absolute truth, we are free to employ compassion and empathy in the space that was once reserved for judgement. When our hearts are joined with others in understanding, not only will there be less strife in our lives and more energy to do what we are on this planet to do, we will also be able to work together more easily and effectively. I am not asking that you accept what you do not believe to be true, only that you hold space for greater understanding. Each of us can benefit from this practice in our work and daily lives as global citizens, cultural diplomats, thought leaders or evolutionary thinkers.

I recently heard a story about a man who was part of a militia. Having been captured as a boy, he had been trained from the time he was a child to fight. When he came of age, he captured a woman, raped her, took her as his property, and they raised a family together. As the years passed and they learned to work together as parents, they opened up to each other, and the man expressed that he didn't want to be a fighter in that situation. He had never had the opportunity to share that with another person. Together they escaped the captivity that imprisoned them both and started a new life. Society sees the fighter, rapist, father and husband as both a victim and villain because all of those things are simultaneously true.

Lesson 25
Love, Joy and Prayer

Inspiration

I align myself with the purity of Love. I am a conduit of this essence. I give my presence and receive undiluted bounty. Love is my match, my decision, my choice, my desire, my alignment, my right and my opportunity. There is no obstacle between Love and me except myself. I let Love dissolve all obstacles that I have created for myself. Love is abundant in its subtle and ever-present perfection. Love is our birthright and the source to which we will return. It is all the spectrums of the rainbow; all that is manifest and unmanifest. It is a force beyond imagination. It is Source. It is not a diminishing resource; it cannot be traded, owned or controlled. It is free and readily available to all. Love does not discriminate. It has no eyes, judgement or requirements. Love is our partner in all things and in all ways if we allow our hearts to be complimented and uplifted by its bounty.

Concept

Prayer is the practice of being inside of the unmanifest. Prayer is the bridge between now and desire. The feeling of Love is an essence that unites our alignment with our highest calling because it is a conduit, which allows for our hearts to be at peace.

When we attune to Love, it is as if we are developing new receptor sites that are matched with this specific vibration. Everything changes: what we see and how we see it, what we say and how we say it, what we hear and how we hear it, generally what we experience and how we experience it. It's as though we are morphing our reality, changing it to reflect something new. Love is an invitation to be a different sort of person, have a different quality of interactions, experience joy in newfound ways and express yourself in ways that feed you. You are shifting the world around you from within, from the way you interact within it.

What if we could choose joy in our lives? When I first started exploring the idea of taking personal responsibility for living in joy, I would contradict this belief by arguing, "How can people who live in extreme poverty, who have lost their home, their health, or their stability choose joy in a time of such pain and suffering?" Then I was given the opportunity to visit internally displaced Palestinian refugees in two different densely populated refugee camps in the Occupied Palestinian Territory of the West Bank. And there, beautifully-hearted people showed me that circumstance does not dictate freedom of spirit. I learned joyfulness in this place from people who had so much to give with the very little that they had.

In the Holy Land of Palestinians and Israelis, Muslims, Jews and Christians, prayer can be an act that divides us or unites us. I believe that the ultimate cause and desire for prayer is Love. Love is not divisive. Love is the sublime power that unifies each of our shared power, privilege, loss and pain. Love holds all; all people, all experiences and all perspectives. Love is non-dualistic.

Practice

Imagine that everything you know to be true exists inside of a bubble: your identity, your memories, knowledge and attachments. Your bubble is a practice space for you to define who you are in reference to all that exists. What exists outside of the bubble is everything else, which is outside of your awareness. There is no tension in this space outside of your bubble: it just IS. All the seeming duality is in perfect balance. Now think of how sheer, malleable and delicate the lining of your bubble is in contrast to the infinite space outside of it. Get curious about what it would feel like to not be confined by the membrane of the bubble that keeps you separate from all that exists. Imagine what it would feel like to burst your bubble and be in unison with Source. Love is a pathway to dismantle the membrane that confines you inside of your bubble.

"Spirit guide me to do, say, act, hear, speak, that which is in my highest alignment." ~ A prayer from A Course in Miracles.

Lesson 26
Falling in Love with Your Beloved Even if You Haven't Yet Met

Inspiration

Beloved, I hold Love that is so explosive that it takes all of my strength to hold on, Love that moves me to crystalline tears of utter joy, Love so raw that it scours my past and opens my future. I welcome Love that is undiluted, uncomplicated and uncompromised, so magical as to unveil new worlds of wonder, potential and possibility. I welcome Love like light touching the sky, like galaxies colliding or hearts merging. Love…

Concept

What does it feel like to Love unconditionally? What does it feel like to be Loved unconditionally? You could begin to tap into the experience of giving and receiving unconditional love through recalling a relationship with a child or a pet.

What if shame ceased to exist and you acknowledge that you are Loved, Lovable and Loving at all times and with all beings? Imagine that you are innocent in the all-knowing embrace of Love. Let yourself succumb to the pure vulnerability of knowing that nothing is wrong with you. Know that you are the highest manifestation of creation, and you are the product of Love. Could you let yourself feel the powerful penetration of that Love into all of you: your mind, your body and your imagination? What if you surrendered to the knowing that you are already Loved beyond your imagination? If you were to summon your beloved playmate inside an energy of being afraid, calloused or disdainful of Love, what kind of vibrational match would you be attracting? Probably not someone that could match you in a higher alignment of Love. It is the flower in full-blooming surrender that calls to the bee. The bee is not wooed by thick bark or a bud tightly bound; it finds its nectar in the blossom that opens itself to the nourishing, life-giving light.

Practice

Hold this in your imagination. I am Love. I am joy. I am you, and you are me. I have always been and always will be. We are bound by the magnetism of our energetic imprint. I live in the knowledge that what I seek is seeking me. We are both beings of the same light, and our love exists beyond the confines of time and space. We may not have met or recognized each other yet, but my higher self, the one that is led by Love, welcomes you. I have the courage, curiosity and commitment to Love, to stay in the divine glory of your being. I am Love. I am joy. I am you, and you are me.

Lesson 27
Devotion

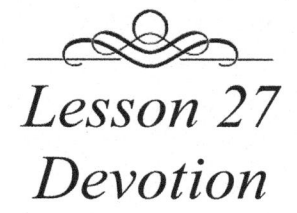

Inspiration

I surrender my heart to you; I give all of myself to you. You are the center of my heart; my breath is yours. My body is your temple. You are the cosmic wave, the center of everything that exists and unmanifest. I feel your breath in the wind and your smile in the sun. You are joy, bountifully overflowing through the hearts of all who open themselves to receive you. You are the essence of life and the fruit of Love. The spiral of your Love is creation. I am you, and you are me. We are the co-creators of this divine plan. I relinquish my knowing to your wisdom. Tell me, show me, guide me; let me be the vessel of your Love. My body is a container for the expression of this Love. It is boundless, beautiful, blissful.

Concept

Devotion can be an act of Love to anything, a beloved, a faith, a belief, a career, an idea, a process of discovery, a practice or a movement. Each of us is so vastly unique that even within a shared practice, individuals can show devotion in a multitude of ways. Devotion is the willingness to give yourself to something that you hold to be greater than yourself. It is something that you choose to become, which is greater than the sum of its parts. It is the desire to present yourself in the best way that you can; to direct your effort, belief and commitment towards something that you hold with dear respect. Devotion often requires discipline, which stems from the word disciple. It is a practice that often takes unwavering commitment, endurance and faith. Devotion is one of the many paths to Love, as it requires a sturdy and surrendered heart. It is the process of surrender that is the catalyst for a blossoming heart. It is the relinquishment of yourself that makes space for Love to fill the void.

Practice

Imagine that you are supported beyond your capacity to understand. Sit down in a comfortable position and imagine that the earth is your anchor. Let yourself feel the gravity of our great provider, Gaia, holding you. Feel how sturdy, abundant and nurturing she is. If you have ever felt unsupported, feel into how vastly supported you are by the enormity and abundance of our planet. Gaia has been providing for us in each moment of our lives. She is the sustainer of life and has provided all of the elements that have supported us, our ancestors and all of life for time immemorial. She does not judge us. Her waters fall from the sky, flow through the rivers, lakes and oceans without assignment or priority of who is nourished by them. Her air and bounty are given without judgement of who uses them. She provides without the demand for compensation. Lean into her. Connect to her strength and ever-present support.

She is holding you and will continue to hold you in any form you take.

Imagine growing a sturdy taproot from the base of your body, which anchors deeply through the crust of the earth, down into the core so that you feel deeply rooted. When you know that you are unshakably grounded, open up the energetic fields of your body, the chakras or energy centers. Begin with the base and move up to your crown. Let each of these energy centers unfurl, expanding in awareness. As you are doing this, let yourself dissolve all thoughts so that you are free from thinking. Allow silence and stillness to be the only awareness.

The greatest surrender can be the greatest devotion. Welcome profound insights during or after this process.

Lesson 28
Lineage, Evolution & Love

Inspiration

Thank you, my grandmothers, for striving to be your best, for improving yourselves and providing the best family that you could for your children. Thank you for loving them, tending to them, nourishing and nurturing them. Thank you for paving the way for me to be here today. Thank you for the health you have bestowed upon me, the history that you have given me and for the stories that have paved the foundation for my experience of this world. Thank you for instilling in me the Love of family, home and lineage. I am here because you were here first. I strive to heal myself and any wounding that has been passed down through the generations. I acknowledge that I am the current fruit of our family's evolution. I persist in freeing myself from any ancestral pain and, in doing so, unravel any pain that has been passed through the generations.

Concept

I have read that trauma can be passed down through DNA. A Google search came up with 18 million results on the topic. It's a provocative thing to think about. Most humans have experienced something difficult. I'm hard-pressed to think of a time or people unaffected by war, displacement or environmental catastrophe. I am not a neuroscientist, so I cannot validate or discredit this possibility. However, I have seen trauma play out in the learned and, or inherited behaviors of most people I have known. I think that it is worthwhile to actively acknowledge that we all have some historical pain that is inherent to us, be it from our DNA, our upbringing, or both. We have to wonder if freeing ourselves from the spiral of our ancestral past can heal our future.

Practice

Imagine that you are standing in a box of mirrors, and you can see a reflection of yourself that stretches into infinity. Imagine that you are standing in that box, but each of the subsequent reflections is one of your predecessors in chronological order. Imagine that each of these beings is truly overjoyed that you exist. Imagine that each generation has evolved past the previous, and you are the one that they have been waiting for. You are their salvation. You have the capacity to acknowledge the collective pain of your lineage and simply let it go. You can choose to heal it by releasing it so that it does not haunt future generations. Know that they are so proud of you for seeing them, and they recognize how powerful and sensitive you are. Their lives were, in essence, to bring you into being and give you all that you need to be successful in your life. They have known that someday one in their lineage would release them from the bond that ties these souls together. See them as far back as you can, feel their Love and joy in knowing that you exist. Know that you are unwinding the karmic ties that bind. Know that you are free, and they are free. Know that they are grateful. They are at peace and want you to be too!

Lesson 29
Tolerance & Justice

Inspiration

"Blessed are the peacemakers, for they will be called children of Heaven." 9th beatitude, Jesus

"Those who are active agents of unity and reconciliation wherever they are. The peace here is not simply the absence of hostilities, an uneasy truce, but a genuine healing and bringing together. We can be peacemakers in our families and homes, in our schools and workplaces, in our places of worship and in all the areas of our society where there is conflict. Peace is inextricably linked with justice. There cannot be peace where there is prejudice, discrimination or exploitation. It would be difficult to find a nicer thing to say about someone than that he or she is a peacemaker. No wonder such people are called children of Heaven." Commentary by the Irish Jesuits at
https://livingspace.sacredspace.ie/oa041/

Concept

The tolerance I speak of here is not passive acceptance. It is more in the vein of active understanding. I use justice as a synonym for healing. Tolerance and justice are both active endeavors. The great leaders of conscience have actively reshaped themselves, their minds, hearts and actions to live more fully in alignment with their beliefs and ideals.

Martin Luther King showed us that Love is courage. When Love challenges hate, it is Love that remains because Love holds moral authority. Change begins with you, your choices, what you demonstrate, what you expect, what you tolerate, what you engage in, what you devote your attention to, what you chose to say or no to, what financial decisions you make and that with which you choose to disengage. The great non-violent leaders who have transformed the world have been successful due to their commitment to their higher selves, their devotional Love and their dedication to advancing the lives of their followers and devotees.

Thich Nhat Hanh, the Dali Lama, Gandhi, Mother Teresa and MLK have been connected to a higher mind through Love and service. This presence gave them the wisdom and strength to stay above fear. Each of these evolutionaries was accessing their higher mind through different access points, but there is continuity in their messages: be active in cultivating change for the betterment of others. There is nothing passive in any of their teachings: use your body, voice, experience, relationships, money, skills and intelligence to work towards liberation, success and an equitable future for all.

In Hinduism, this is called Seva, the active process of working towards serving the healing of society. There is momentum in this work. The more willing you are to actively shape the experience in your life by becoming accountable to yourself, being aware of the outcome of your decisions, consciously choosing what you want to invite into your life and acknowledging that you are participating in creating that for yourself, the easier it will become to live in alignment and ease in Love. We become wiser with each breath, each step and each moment when we devote ourselves to the service of others and the greater good.

Justice can be something that heals communities affected by violation. My father was a judge, and between the ages of 8 and 12, I spent a month of each of my summers in a criminal courtroom. I have been thinking about justice for a long time.

In its highest potential, justice is a way for us to see one another's perspective. It is a way for us to harmonize the various interpretations of a shared event. It is an opportunity to mend, heal, be heard, understood and recognized. Justice does not necessarily need to be punitive; it can act as a bridge to healing the mind, body and community of both the victim and the perpetrator. Justice is a mechanism through which the difficulties and challenges that are inevitable in the human experience can be recognized, mended and resolved.

Justice is an avenue to Love because it can trigger our primal need to be validated while simultaneously providing us with an opportunity to stretch the possibilities of our compassion and sympathies to understand something that is not innate to our own experience. This mixture of vulnerability in concurrence with the possibility for expansiveness makes for a potentially transformative heart-opening experience.

Love is a radically different energy than hate. Love is expansive. Hate is contractive. Both are universal forces that have a depth from which one can pull energy. However, the resonance of Love in the body is obviously much more harmonious, peaceful, relaxing and rejuvenating, while hate is frenetic, isolating and stressful. You can find Love through peace and vice versa, but you cannot be at peace in hate.

Tolerance and justice are not necessarily compatible. We should not tolerate destruction, greed, disempowerment, discrimination, misinformation, disrespect and violence. However, we are far better off when we are tolerant of each other. When we can see others in their innocence, we can have compassion for them and maybe even understand how they got to where they are now. Maybe we can see that there is no malice in their actions, but simply unconsciousness. Malice certainly exists in the world. I choose to first assume that malice is not one's intention.

Practice

Ask yourself what peace means to you. Set a timer and sit with this question for 5 minutes. See what words, feelings, memories or sensations arise. Then ask yourself what does tolerance mean to you? Give yourself another 5 minutes to ponder how it looks and feels. What does justice mean? Set a timer for another 5 minutes and sit with the question. Find out how you may have previously experienced justice and if there is room to change that experience into something different. Now give yourself a few minutes to consider each of the following questions. What does the intersection of Love and peace look like? What does the intersection of Love and tolerance look like? What does the intersection of Love and justice look like?

Lesson 30
Shedding Layers

Inspiration

I am the one who I have been waiting for. I truly and deeply thank myself for showing up for me, being present for me, Loving me, acknowledging me and seeing all my best intentions. No one else can possibly care for my heart with as much care as I can provide for myself. I understand myself as no one else ever will. I am innocent. I forgive myself for my own judgements. I have always been perfect, exactly the way that I am.

Concept

Imagine that you are speaking to a younger version of yourself. Recognize that no one will ever know you the way that you know yourself, so no one will ever Love you the way that you can love yourself.

When I do this exercise, I realize that as much as I love my daughter, Izabela and know her better than any person alive, I will never be able to understand her experience the way that I understand my own. Her experience is her own, as is mine.

Each of us is so unique that when we extend compassion toward the younger version of ourselves, it is more profound than anything another person could ever offer.

Practice

Get into a comfortable, quiet space and begin to breathe deeply. Breathe into every corner of your body until you feel relaxed. You can practice the body scan from chapter 8. Imagine a time that you would like to interact with your past self. Maybe there is an event that you would like to understand better, heal or confront. Imagine that the younger version of yourself stands at the other side of a door. Give the door color and texture. With an open mind and an open heart, turn the knob and open the door. What does this person look like? How does it feel to see yourself at this time? You can share words of wisdom, comfort, advise, or ask for any information that until this point has been unattainable. You can develop a lifelong practice of healing and better understanding your own experience. Each of us is a vast warehouse of stored information.

Lesson 31
Spirals of Refinement and Release

Inspiration

As I go inward, ever deeper, I peer into the inner folds of my being. I softly and gently untether the bound fascia of my inner workings. As I go deeper, the contraction is more condensed and what is held in the precious space in between becomes less and less necessary, the pockets of resistance between my identity and my essence. I find that my center is Source. And when I find center, I spiral out, knowing that my continual refinement is the concentration of every moment in my life. From there, I expand to see where I end, and infinity begins. I find that I am infinity.

Concept

Imagine that our lives are patterned like the spiral of a shell or of the many fractals found in nature. Contemplate that there is no origin and no end. It is simply about the process of following the spiral. As the never-ending spiral splays out, it leads us to remember our constantly evolving expansion. Our evolution is in surrender, increasing the space in our bodies as we become bigger and more unified with all that is. The spiral outward is manifestation, spaciousness, surrender of ego, elimination of identity, unification with all that exists. This spiral exists for all of us and is continuous. It does not stop whether we recognize it or not.

The inward spiral exists simultaneously. One is not better than the other; they coexist. The spiral inward is the refinement of our understanding. It is the message, the dance, the reformatting of information into understandable, digestible, usable skill, potency and understanding. The word here is refinement, information transformed into ever-increasingly useful and accessible information.

Practice

Imagine that you are at the center of a spiral. You are the median point. The spirals within you spin both inward and outward simultaneously. Imagine holding both of these currents inside of you. It may, however, be easier to choose one direction at first and imagine that before revisiting the opposite direction.

For instance, imagine all that binds you into the perfect creature that you are, is becoming more and more crisp and clear as it spirals into ever smaller concentric circles. All that you have harnessed into the masterpiece of you becomes condensed into a richer and more savory rue. The matter that makes up your structure becomes more defined, decocted, potent. The expanse in between gently gives up its space for only the most valuable elements of who you are. Let's say that the spiral boils your essence down to the most essential elements, the aspects of you that are most important as your contribution to this life and this time. Feel into this and give yourself permission to find out what makes up the essence of you. If your existence were boiled down to one drop, what potency exists in that essence? What does it feel like to release your identity as it becomes minuscule? Take five long deep breaths into this place and see what exists here.

Now, as you spiral into the infinite expanse, how much of yourself can you let go of, surrender, relinquish? How does it feel to become as large as a car, a house, an apartment building, a city, a region, a country, an ocean, a planet, a solar system, a galaxy, a universe? Take five long deep breaths as you expand your awareness of yourself into the vastness of your potential.

You can certainly continue beyond five breaths for as long as this exercise is offering new or valuable information. Once you feel comfortable in the expanse of both directions separately, you can work towards holding both simultaneously.

Lesson 32
Fear as a Guide

Inspiration

Song – Beautiful, Bountiful, Blissful,
https://youtu.be/nqFZTmXyddI

I am Beautiful, I am Bountiful, I am Blissful, I am...

Concept

What is fear? Primal fears include rejection, abandonment, betrayal, violation, loss, failure, guilt (self-doubt), engulfment, pain (physical or emotional), death (unknowing, change) and lack of control. As powerful as these concepts are in detouring us from our purpose, I question the wisdom of crafting decisions based on the avoidance of them. If we create our lives from the prism of fear, we are going to also experience the outcomes of our lives within that prism.

As a young woman, I noticed that when I made a decision based on fear, the decision felt obscured, like it wasn't lit by truth, or there was critical information missing. I played with this idea a lot as I traveled through Mexico and Central America on my own in 1999 and 2000.

I noticed that when I made a decision that was guided by fear, it felt as though that decision was always limiting. There was a retractive quality to it versus an expansive one. I practiced reframing decisions into what felt right and found that my heart and intuition provided a profoundly better compass than my mind, which would often find a reason for me not to even make a decision. Fear is a powerful tool that our ego uses to distract us from our intuition and renders us paralyzed if we surrender to it.

The fear that I have struggled with most has been rejection. When I had finally experienced enough of the lessons about rejection, I prayed to be illuminated to my blind spots, the limiting beliefs that I just couldn't see. I was tired of my friends telling me that there was nothing wrong with me. I realized that I was creating the same drama for myself time and again. I knew that I could not change the world to conform to my needs or patiently wait for something that I wanted. I knew that I was the common denominator, and I alone had the power to change my experience. I finally figured out it was my experience of rejection that was the source of my pain, so I confronted it. I was so fed up with my recurring story that I faced the dragon head-on. I was not going to reject myself and my need for a resolution. I gently gave rejection back to its source, which was not me. I gave up my addiction to rejection, my relationship with it, my attachment to it. I released the power that it had over me. It felt like I not only confronted the dragon, but I went inside of it. I needed to feel all of it so that it no longer had any control over me. I needed to feel the fire inside of its belly so that I knew that I no longer had anything to be afraid of. I was so radically done with the pain of my fear that it felt like I beheaded the dragon from the inside.

Practice

Imagine something that bothers you. You don't have to delve into your core wound on this first round. Maybe just something that has been frustrating to you recently. When you identify the feeling, peel away the story and just sit with the feeling. Really indulge in what that feeling is. Go underneath the judgement. Go through the right and wrong, leave the moral constructs of it behind. What is the feeling? Is it one of the primal fears: rejection, abandonment, betrayal, violation, loss, failure, guilt (self-doubt), engulfment, pain (physical or emotional), death (un-knowing, change), or lack of control? Have you felt this specific feeling before? Is it related to other experiences? Did this feeling begin somewhere else? Once you confront these questions, you will find that the frustration that you are feeling is most likely a fracture of your greatest lesson, your greatest fear. Remember Lesson 19, Looking into the Shadows. What if you confronted that fear head-on? What if your belief, understanding, illusion around that fear was actually more powerful than the outcome of the fear? Imagine being able to resolve, dissolve, evolve fear into a comical, powerless, ridiculous thought. How much spaciousness and emotional expanse would you have available to make more coherent, informed choices based on deeper rationality?

Love is a higher vibration and has the power to heal. It is intractable. Love cannot be denied. It is a force that has no equivalent. Love's obstacle is fear. Imagine if you continued to choose Love over fear again and again in every circumstance and at every opportunity.

Lesson 33
Love Does Not Need to be Passive Love Can Be Fierce

Inspiration

I own ALL of my power

I am not scared or intimidated by the ferocity of Love that pulses through my body

I am filled with flower and flame

I am bold and relentless

I hold courage and strength in the grounding of my Love

I am committed to using all the strengths, skills and vulnerabilities that life has taught me

I have been empowered by all of the experiences that I have had

I am not afraid of my own power

I can use this power to support all that I do

There is nothing wrong with me accessing all parts of myself

I am full of emotional fuel, and I chose to launch into the potent agent of my greatest possibility

Concept

There was a time when I was very challenged by friends saying they would pray for peace. I judged this as too passive and not active enough. I have been one to choose to be more outwardly expressive in my actions towards building a more peaceful and equitable world. However, as I have wizened, I see that there is true value in redirecting energy and intention in envisioning the emergence of a more equitable world.

I have to validate the aikido effect of not fighting force with force but of allowing force to consume itself. That said, the peace warriors who have most effectively shaped recent history have been those who are outspoken with the conviction of the divine behind them. Among them are Dr. Martin Luther King Jr., a Baptist minister, Mahatma Gandhi, a devout Hindu, Mother Teresa, a Catholic nun, Thich Nhat Hanh, a Buddhist monk and the Dali Lama, the spiritual and political leader of Tibetan Buddhism. These individuals are forceful in their determination to create change through their connection to the potency of universal truth - to the power of Love of something far greater than themselves, humanity. These notable peace warriors have consciously utilized connection to unabridged, universal Love. They have all soared in their work because it is not the ego that they serve; it is the recognition of, and devotion to, the best that humanity has to offer.

The following is an excerpt from a piece that I wrote in 2016 called *Ego, Power, Evolution*.

It is us, the imagining cells of the great butterfly, that can see the way. We have the power and determination to pivot into peace, collaboration and shared humanity. We are waking up to alternatives, channeling the future, cultivating beauty and blossoming hope.

We can choose to affect change through cooperation, communication, investigation and mobilization. We are not feeble. We are not passive. We have the power of choice. Who will win the conflict of consciousness, the most vile expression of our species or our shared humanity?

If you have found yourself here, I invite you to rise up to the potency of yourself, your life and your contribution to this time. I ask that you live in the enormity of your potential, big and bold, act in determination and pride, armed with conviction and pride. Let us ripple the essence of our vision, our light, our possibility into every crevice of our lives.

In each breath, each step and each moment, we are creating a place where Love dominates fear, hope destroys oppression, and unity conquers separation. Love is strength; evolution is power!

Practice

The exercise of throwing Love bombs is pretty fun. It does not take compassion or understanding. This practice can be used in frustration or in tenderness. It is an explosive force. I imagine these Love bombs as actual balls of fire emanating out of me. They are from a source that is devoid of judgement. I came up with the concept during periods of frustration when I could not understand someone or something. Instead of stewing in my discontent, I would just cultivate enough Love and throw it at that with which I did not agree or understand.

What would it feel like if we were able to throw Love bombs rather than harmful ones? What if we could ground ourselves in knowing that we do not make ourselves safer when hurting others? Only by recognizing each other's fundamental truths can we understand that we are all a family of interconnected beings.

How will we change the world that we live in for the better? Action, yes! Perhaps the actions that we take are not enough. We must use all the senses with which we are inherently graced. We must do what calls us, what we are good at and that which we are inspired to do with a heart of devotion to something greater than ourselves. As we wake, work, breathe and sleep, we can engage ourselves fully, using our hearts, minds, experiences and passion for creating an existence where we all have space to live in a peaceful, safe and fulfilling future. It is not a net sum loss to share. It is a net sum gain to live amongst all of the other inhabitants of earth peacefully and respectfully.

I have no delusions about the existence of fear and greed in the human condition. Looking at it, acknowledging it, and overcoming it is the work that makes us more intentional about how we show up in the world. I do not believe in spiritually bypassing the experience of confronting fear and the lessons therein. We must access a buffet of experiences to nourish what we long for, a deeper connection to Source and Love. All of us, including the change-makers I previously mentioned, live in a messy world of discord and disappointment. However, it is how we wield our experience that is the key that will open the door to creating intention, meaning, understanding and advancement of these experiences.

When you are confused, agitated or feeling defeated, imagine throwing out Love bombs. It could sometimes feel like an aggressive action, but with clear intention, it can burn through the confusion and the illusion of separation. Imagine a situation that makes your heart race with uncertainty. Open your mind and heart and give your agitation to the flame of Love.

Allow yourself the space to suspend judgement for this exercise. Release whatever hurt or frustration you may feel and hold that situation in your heart, acknowledging that it is something that exists whether you are upset about it or not. Ask yourself if there is a different way you can observe this experience. Give yourself the opportunity to truly listen.

What if each of us was able to live in a world that was less charged with the stress of judgement and need for control? What if we could teach each other this practice? What if this new consciousness spread like wildfire across the globe to encompass all peoples and cultures? What would that world look like?

Lesson 34
Community

Inspiration

"Set your life on fire and seek those who fan your flames." ~Rumi

Concept

Community is any group of people that share space, interests, attitudes or goals; a sense of commonality, fellowship, comradery, companionship. It's like an engine that we can use to generate energy, share ideas, to learn, to help us hold our pain, share in effort and lend support. Community holds us when we are weak and when we are strong. Community is an extension or reflection of ourselves, allowing us to better understand who we really are. Our communities know us best and can reflect when we are out of our own alignment. Have you ever felt like everywhere you go, there you are? If you are being authentic, you will magnetize towards other authentic people. Likewise, if you are controlling, you will magnetize towards other controlling people.

We are like bees that resonate in the same hive. Community creates collective experience. We all know the saying coined by Jim Rohn, "We are the average of the five people we spend the most time with." If we change ourselves, we affect the people around us and vice versa.

Community is a safe space to experiment with who we are. It is a lab to investigate where our triggers lie and how we choose to deal with such unearthed information. We need community to give us feedback on our reactions to situations. Community provides a container for our exploration. A place to figure out what is ours and what belongs to another.

Often people have multiple communities that can reflect various facets of an individual's personality. Community is there as a vehicle for us to lift each other up as we inspire each other to be the best version of ourselves.

We all deserve this! One of the most mutually nourishing things that one individual can ask another is, "How can I help you?" Seva, or devotional service, can be sharing an asset, a compliment or a smile. We are on this planet together: humans, plants and animals. We are in the struggle for dignity, shared humanity and the evolution of consciousness together. No one is a super(s)hero alone. When we work together to support each other's efforts, we are a self-perpetuating, self-elevating network, a biome that is greater than the sum of its parts.

A friend told me once that when she began to notice all the thoughts that were her conditioning, she realized that many of those thoughts didn't actually belong to her. They were a consequence of her patterning. She would simply say "back to sender" and energetically unfurl the thought from her being and send it back to its source.

Practice

What would it feel like if you were able to be seen in your entirety by others? What does it feel like to be surrounded by people who understand your authentic self, to feel connected to people who want to nourish your talents and aspirations, who are curious about the gifts you have to offer, who respect you and want to be in alignment with you? Sink into how that feels. What does it look like? Who is there? What is your offering?

Lesson 35
Balance of Tension

Inspiration

Love is a mystery, void of beginning or end. Each of us is an expression of this infinite fractal, unique in our size, shape, color, texture and the speed with which we unfurl ourselves. It is a continual interplay of emergence into the collective. Light, energy and metamorphosis are the catalysts of life, and Love is the amplifier. Here nothing exists that is stagnant. It is not fixed, permanent or unchanging. Love is like the seasons, which bloom, retreat, give and receive. Like the cycles of nature, Love is fluid in its seasons, reminding us of the potency of birth, destruction and mortality. It ebbs and flows as we flex and contract in our needs and desires.

As romantic Love changes over time, so does the Love of family, community and self. Love is most powerful when it is held gently without control. A hand will crush a rose if it is held too tightly. Love cannot dominate, be contained or manipulated. It is the alchemy of Love that gives us wings. It is ever-present, lives in all things, at all times, in all spaces. It is greater than our collective mind can fathom. It is the mirror of the heart that opens to receive it. The more surrendered the heart, the more Love is able to penetrate, flood, imbue the recipient. When we deceive ourselves into thinking that we can control Love, that is when Love shows us that it is a constant that will only bow to our best intentions and our highest good. Our bodies and minds are hourglasses through which experiences pass, but Love is the source of the sand and the glass that contains it. Knowing that Love is everywhere and a part of everything, we can surrender to knowing that Love is the connective fabric that binds us.

Concept

Love is not something that needs to be reserved for specific people. I recently saw a colleague whom I respect at the grocery store, and I could feel a deep affection that left us both shining from recognizing each other's humanity.

Jealousy cannot demand that you refrain from sharing authentic Love. Love is abundant; it only becomes diminished when we contain it. By controlling another's ability to Love abundantly, a partner can actually train their beloved to shut down their capacity to give and receive Love. This does not serve the relationship or the individuals in it. Trying to control or place parameters on someone else's Love disallows them to fully be themselves or express the innate goodness that only they can share with this world. The more we allow others to Love in their unique expression, the more they will be able to Love us and the world that surrounds us all. We cannot demand that one person's Love belongs solely to us. If we have chosen to Love a person, we should value their Love as a light so valuable that it is essential in the illumination of this world we share. Love is our divine right and our greatest asset, although it can become stagnant when we inhibit its expression.

Practice

It is the surrender that makes giving and receiving Love so poignant and ecstatic. Practice giving people compliments. Give them without attachment to receiving expected responses. Offer them in good faith. Find something you can appreciate about someone else. As long as it continues to feel authentic, continue to experiment with this as often as you can. See how it makes you feel to not have attachment to the reaction. This is a practice, so start slow and build on the new pathways you are developing in your brain.

See if you can share something on the edge of your comfort zone without being attached to the recipient's response. Maybe this is an opportunity to check in with someone about a shared experience by asking, "How did you perceive that?" You may express a dislike as, "I'm not comfortable with..." See if you can stay unattached to the response that you get from the other person while staying in a place of Love. Stay relaxed, curious and non-judgmental. Try to stay in a non-reactive place of Loving calm as you receive their response. The key word here is authentic. Otherwise, this can come across as condescending, manipulative or even worse, as projecting a lack of sincere feeling.

When you tell someone that you Love them or appreciate them, tell them why. Give them an example of something that they did or said, such as a gesture that you noticed, whether it was something significant or minor. Let the person you appreciate know that you are paying attention to the goodness that they are exuding.

Lesson 36
I Am Enough

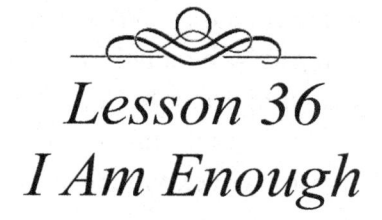

Inspiration

I am not a body having a spiritual experience. I am a spirit having a human experience. Knowing this, I acknowledge the enormity of my being. There is no lack, there is no shame, there are no missing parts. I am an amalgamation of all of my experiences, "good" and "bad." I am whole because all these experiences have given me insight, resilience and acceptance. I was whole when I was born. I have been whole in every moment of my life, even the moments when I was unaware of my wholeness (holiness). I am a part of the wholeness that is Love, which unites us and permeates all things.

Concept

When we realize that we are all vessels of Love, using our physical bodies as tools to experience and transmit this information, we understand that there could not possibly be anything lacking. Each of us is equipped with the perfect transmission tool for us to be in a direct relationship with Source, Love.

If you are reading these words, Source energy has conspired to get you here. Your body is a cauldron of Love. Love does not need you to be anything other than you are in this moment. You are perfect because you are. Love has been your greatest ally in each moment of your life. It has held you in all that you have experienced. You have always been and will always be innocent in Love. Love is your birthright.

Practice

Imagine that you are a droplet of pure water, existing as separate only because you are not merged within the ocean, lake or other body of water. When you are merged with all of the other droplets within a body of water, you cannot differentiate between where you end and where another droplet begins. You are inseparable, unified. There is no droplet of water that is better than another; each is perfect in its shared essence. A droplet does not desire to be a different droplet. Each droplet is perfection and an essential ingredient to life on this planet. You are this water droplet. You are a part of the perfect balance of what exists here and now. You are a part of the pattern, a piece of the puzzle; without you, with all of your flaws and talents, the collective would not be experiencing itself in the same way. You are a beat in the rhythm, a color in the spectrum. The impact of your existence is immeasurable.

The fact that you exist means that there is a purpose for you to exist.

What does it feel like to know that you are enough, that there is nothing missing, that you are whole? Surrender to that feeling. Let yourself be fully held, encapsulated in the knowing that Love has got you. There is nothing that you can do to be rejected by Love. You are innocent to Love. The source of Love is within you and is the connective force between all that exists. You are both the source of Love and its vessel.

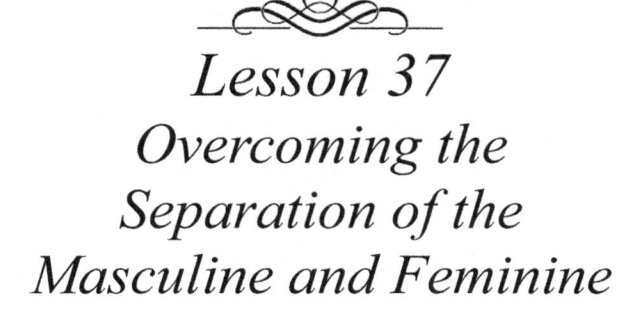

Lesson 37
Overcoming the Separation of the Masculine and Feminine

Inspiration

"You come to us from another world

from beyond the stars

and the void of space

transcendent, pure of unimaginable beauty

bringing with you the essence of Love

you transform all who are touched by you

mundane concerns, troubles and sorrows dissolve in your presence

bringing joy to ruler and ruled

to peasant and king

you bewilder us with your grace

all evils transform into goodness

you are the master alchemist

you light the fire of Love in earth and sky

in the heart and soul of every being

through your loving, existence and non-existence merge

all opposites unite

all that is profane becomes sacred again"

~ Rumi

Concept

What if we didn't need another to make us happy? If we are fully content in our lives, then those who show up to give us love and companionship become the whipped cream on top of a vessel already filled to the brim. Can you imagine the joy you could feel with a person if you didn't need that person to complete you? What if you could revel in this individual simply being in your life? You could thoroughly appreciate the relationship without an attachment to whether another acts out your script. If you are already full, no one can take that away from you; one can only add flavor to the mix.

I once had a dream about a man who was fervently trying to do his perceived job as his family's caretaker. He was trying so hard to do his best to provide and keep them safe and happy. It was his true desire to be the best he could be in this role. Although, the symbolism in the dream inferred that he just wasn't able to be all that was expected of him by himself, societal norms and his family. He was overwhelmed, despondent and incapacitated by the enormity of not having the capacity of being enough. This dream was memorable for me as it illuminated the pressure that patriarchal thought places on men when they don't feel free to ask for or rely on support from their partners and family. It allowed me to see that both men and women are the victims of this outdated paradigm. And only through communication, vulnerability and the authentic desire to support each other in our strengths and weaknesses will we have equality in our relationships.

Practice

This exercise can be done alone, spoken to yourself in the mirror, with a partner, mate, spouse, friend, or even witnessed by more than one person in a group. Make sure to have plenty of time for this exercise and quiet space to take in the words that are being spoken. Speak these words out loud. Take your time. Feel what you are saying. Convey your sincerity in reciting them.

"I'm sorry if you are experiencing confusion right now. I understand that you may not know how to act or be as a (wo)man in this dynamically changing time. How can I support you?"

"I acknowledge the young (wo)man or child in you that was conditioned in a patriarchal system. I see that you are a sensitive being who needs Love and support and that it is difficult for you to pretend that you know what's best, to posture as confident, and to be perceived as unsure."

"I want to know you and see every dimension of you. I am willing to be patient and wait till all of you is comfortable showing yourself to me."

"You do not need to fit into a mold. I am curious to learn about the unique eccentricities that belong only to you."

"Do you trust me enough to be radically honest with yourself and me in emerging as the most divine person that you can be?"

"You are not losing control. The parts of you that are no longer necessary are becoming obsolete to make room for the true you. You are emerging from a chrysalis into a butterfly."

"You can change the world by changing your heart."

"I want to walk in this world with you in our full potency."

"Your wounds are the wounds of humanity, and by healing yourself, you are healing a piece of the greater whole."

"I completely trust that you are doing your best. I see the best in you."

"I believe in the good in you, I see the good in you, I have trust and faith that the goodness in you will prevail."

Lesson 38
Heartbreak

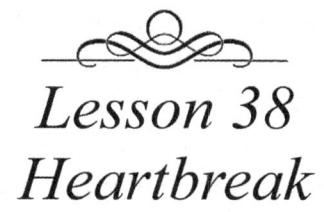

Inspiration

"How shall my heart be unsealed unless it be broken? Only great sorrow or great joy can reveal your truth. If you would be revealed, you must either dance naked in the Sun or carry your cross." ~Kahlil Gibran

Concept

I am shattered open. My heart is raw and exposed. There is no protection between me and the full-throttle ride of reality. The pain of existence exposes me to the presence of now. There is nothing between now and the void. I am cracked open, a seed that has been exposed to the sun's piercing light. I am vulnerable and in a precious state of receptivity. In this space, I let the light in. I receive through the wounds, cracks and scars. I know that the pain of heartbreak is the fertilizer that will nourish the next phase of my relationship to divine Love. My ego and identity are slipping away. My attachments to the past and the future become meaningless. I am in the riptide of self-actualization. With each breath, each step and each moment, I am blossoming into my new awareness, guided by Love.

Therein lies the purity, vulnerability, the essence of Love, the catalyst for divine Love. It is when we are broken open that we succumb to the subtlety of innocence. It is a time when we are fluid, raw and fertile. In the enormity of feeling, seismic shifts are possible; cataclysmic shifts that take us into the underworld only to spit us back out on the opposite side of existence. Commitment to staying in divine Love can be a guide through the underworld. This is the moment when the heat, pressure and combustion can turn coal into a diamond.

Practice

Breathe. Just breathe… Take long, deep breaths and exhale everything that feels stuck inside of your body. Imagine that you are letting go of the old thoughts, patterns, expectations—all those thoughts that loop over and over again in your head and act as traps into messy, unproductive thinking.

Tell those thoughts that you no longer have space for them. Let yourself become an empty vessel. Keep yourself as open and empty as you possibly can. Let yourself rest in this place where your thoughts do not control you.

The old patterns are useless to you now. They no longer have authority over your mind, body or awareness. Living in your ego will continue to deceive you. It is the trickster that conspires to keep you away from Love.

Let yourself be totally present in this moment; there is nothing to do next, everything that has been done is past. This is the only moment that exists. Be inside of it.

Let yourself feel the simple essence of Love. Give that gift to yourself without a story attached to it. Let Love be your ally and companion. Untether yourself from the attachment to what it should be or what you want it to be. The only thing that is important in this moment is for you to allow yourself to feel the universal, ecstatic bliss of Love from its source, which can never be given or taken away by another human.

Love can be a constant companion, a compass continuing to point you in the direction of your true north. Love is freedom, freedom is unity, unity is Love.

Epilogue

Ultimately, this book is intended to be a resource for radical Love, liberated awareness and enlightened living. When we acknowledge that we have a choice in each moment to decide whether to live in harmony within ourselves, in our lives and on our planet, then we can take responsibility for our collective decision making about who we want to be and how we show up. Do we want to live now and into the future as divided, fragmented individuals committed to a belief that someone must be wrong for the other to be right? Will we choose to live in the belief that we can't have a healthy planet while simultaneously having jobs, health and security? We have the freedom to decide whether we want to create and live in a world of cooperative advantage, where we move beyond net sum gains and losses, beyond the outdated illusion of winners and losers.

When we guide our decisions based on Love, then we are being that of which all religions speak, the harmony in which nature exists. When we realize that we *are* nature and that we must abide by the intrinsic models nature has provided, we are saying yes to the balance that will bring us into Eden.

When we say yes to Love, how does that change the framework for conflict, resource extraction, monetary and media manipulation? How does that change the way that we care for ourselves, our children and our parents, how we tend the land, the animals, or how we use, distribute and dispose of resources?

What would it look like if we lived in a world where our political, medical and educational leaders were more beholden to a sense of Love of humanity, guided by a current of goodness, over the thirst for greed and a quest for power? I envision a day when we make laws with Love in our hearts.

The idea of living IN Love is non-dualistic and abundant. There is not an owner, a leader, or a finite source. It is available to all people, in all places, at all times. It is an infinite source of energy that can be tapped into individually simply through the awareness and desire to do so. We must collectively create alternatives to war and stay committed to peaceful solutions until these alternatives become the new paradigm.

Love is not someone or something that we can impress upon another, require, demand or even expect. It is a choice. If we want to live in Love, that is a decision only we can make for ourselves. Others around us can appreciate, reject or even learn from our cultivation of this Source energy.

Love is the path that can lead us to create a more cooperative world. We cannot expect others to imagine this world for us. This is our time to live into the boldness of change. We must face ourselves and our future with the commitment to bring our greatest selves to the challenges that exist today. As Alice Walker said, "We are the ones that we have been waiting for."

A friend once told me the difference between the revolutionary spirit of the 1960s and the evolutionary spirit of today is that we are currently changing things with our hearts and intellect, not with the clenched fists and weapons of the past. Today we will prevail with our hearts and minds open, together, undivided.

Barbara Marx Hubbard taught that the human species is currently in a major evolutionary period. She said that we are shifting into "Homo Amore Universalis," birthing into an evolutionary period equipped with evolutionary thinking. Please see Barbara Marx Hubbard *Introducing the New Human.* https://youtu.be/1yqEa7ZaJ10

We have had many examples of individuals throughout history who were thought leaders, visionaries and non-conformists; those who have broken molds and proven what is possible if we begin to question the confines of reality, which have previously restrained and conditioned us.

We must individually contend with where we place the value of our time, effort and consciousness. What decisions are we making based on historical patterns and feedback loops? Are we ready to burst the bubble of I in order to live in the shared understanding of US?

It is the practice of becoming.

Maybe Love becomes the universal language or currency. Maybe our identity is reflected in how much Love we can feel and emit. This is experimental thinking, but Love is innate to each of us. It is my hope that by giving expression to these ideas, we can choose to neutralize inequality and stabilize our social, political and planetary ecology.

Additional Resources

A letter from Albert Einstein to his daughter: on The Universal Force of Love

Albert Einstein (14 March 1879 – 18 April 1955) is perhaps best known for being a theoretical physicist and for receiving the 1921 Nobel Prize in Physics "for his services to Theoretical Physics." A lesser-known fact about arguably one of the most intelligent men of modern times is that he was also a prolific sender of personal notes and letters upon his own personalized letterhead.

In the late 1980s, Einstein's daughter Lieserl donated 1,400 letters written by Einstein to the Hebrew University. The text of one of them is reproduced below for you. Having been sent by Einstein to his daughter, this letter shows a very different side to Einstein's personality and his outlook on the world.

"When I proposed the theory of relativity, very few understood me, and what I will reveal now to transmit to mankind will also collide with the misunderstanding and prejudice in the world.

I ask you to guard the letters as long as necessary, years, decades until society is advanced enough to accept what I will explain below.

There is an extremely powerful force that, so far, science has not found a formal explanation. It is a force that includes and governs all others and is even behind any phenomenon operating in the universe and has not yet been identified by us. This universal force is LOVE.

When scientists looked for a unified theory of the universe, they forgot the most powerful unseen force. Love is Light that enlightens those who give and receive it. Love is gravity because it makes some people feel attracted to others. Love is power because it multiplies the best we have and allows humanity not to be extinguished in their blind selfishness. Love unfolds and reveals. For love, we live and die. Love is God, and God is Love.

This force explains everything and gives meaning to life. This is the variable that we have ignored for too long, maybe because we are afraid of love because it is the only energy in the universe that man has not learned to drive at will.

To give visibility to love, I made a simple substitution in my most famous equation. If instead of $E = mc^2$, we accept that the energy to heal the world can be obtained through love multiplied by the speed of light squared, we arrive at the conclusion that love is the most powerful force there is because it has no limits.

After the failure of humanity in the use and control of the other forces of the universe that have turned against us, it is urgent that we nourish ourselves with another kind of energy...

If we want our species to survive, if we are to find meaning in life, if we want to save the world and every sentient being that inhabits it, love is the one and only answer.

Perhaps we are not yet ready to make a bomb of love, a device powerful enough to entirely destroy the hate, selfishness and greed that devastate the planet.

However, each individual carries within them a small but powerful generator of love whose energy is waiting to be released.

When we learn to give and receive this universal energy, dear Lieserl, we will have affirmed that love conquers all, is able to transcend everything and anything because love is the quintessence of life.

I deeply regret not having been able to express what is in my heart, which has quietly beaten for you all my life. Maybe it's too late to apologize, but as time is relative, I need to tell you that I love you and thanks to you, I have reached the ultimate answer!"

Your father,

Albert Einstein

Made in the USA
Monee, IL
16 February 2022